# MY FATHER, THE VILLAIN

# MY FATHER, THE VILLAIN
## THE LIFE AND TIMES OF MADAN PURI

LT COL KAMLESH PURI

# BLOOMSBURY
NEW DELHI • LONDON • OXFORD • NEW YORK • SYDNEY

First published in India 2015

ISBN 978 93 854 3619 2
2 4 6 8 10 9 7 5 3 1

Bloomsbury Publishing India Pvt. Ltd
DDA Complex, LSC Building No.4
Second Floor, Pocket C – 6 & 7, Vasant Kunj
New Delhi 110070
www.bloomsbury.com

Typeset by Manmohan Kumar
Printed and bound in India by Gopsons Papers Ltd

To find out more about our authors and books visit www.bloomsbury.com. Here you will find extracts, author interviews, details of forthcoming events and the option to sign up for our newsletters.

This book is dedicated to my late wife, Renuka Puri, who left me two wonderful daughters and eternal memories of our forty-five years together on this earth.

# CONTENTS

# PREFACE

Two years after the death of my beloved wife Renuka in 2005 after a long illness, I decided to write a book about the Sindhi community, so that Renuka's grandchildren would know more about their wonderful grandmother. In this connection I met well-known author Lata Jagtiani, who promised to help me in my research work on Sindhis. When I mentioned that my late father was Madan Puri, her husband Manek Premchand, who writes extensively on Bollywood music, said that Madan Puri was a very popular actor of the sixties and seventies and I should write about him not only as an actor, but also as his son. To find out more about my father's film career I needed to meet and interview as many as possible of my father's ageing colleagues and friends, and time was running out. I put the Sindhi manuscript on hold.

My daughters, Kanchan and Sonal were sixteen and twelve respectively when their *daadu* passed away on 13 January 1985. They have good memories of him. One day I told one of my grandsons that the man in the movie he was watching was my father, and his great-grandfather. He could not comprehend the concept of great-grandfathers! Perhaps he also found it hard to grasp that he was watching someone on screen who was no longer alive. I remembered this incident when I interviewed Raj Kumar Kohli in connection with this book, for he said, 'Madanji and other actors are lucky. Future generations will be able to see them as they looked. We, who are the moviemakers, will end up as pictures on the wall to be dusted and garlanded two or three times a year.'

When I began this biography I had no idea that I was writing about a famous man, though the crowds at his funeral should have been an indication. It was a revelation to discover that he was considered an excellent and prolific actor as well as being a popular and respected member of the film community. In the process of learning more about my father as an actor I also rediscovered him as a parent, and found that the ethics he applied to his profession were equally strong in his private life.

This book is about that great human being.

# FOREWORD

Think of any film you like, and consider what is it that you remember the most. More often than not, it will be the stars, the story and the music. Perhaps the director is someone you admire. You may even remark upon its technical finesse—the photography, the stunts. But rarely, if ever, does anyone pay any attention to the film's supporting cast. When did you last spend time thinking about who played the character roles in a block buster?

But without these character actors, a film could fall flat. However charismatic the lead actor may be, without the support of others around him, he would be a uni-dimensional figure. Character actors, especially those who play smaller roles with skill, are very precious. Directors know their value and importance in lending depth to a story.

Madan Puri was one such actor. He brought immense conviction to his roles. Whether as a suave gangland boss or a thug, and, later in life, as a kindly old uncle or a grandfather, Madan Puri held the viewer's attention, even while sharing the screen with the biggest superstar. He blends efficiently into the demands of the scene, rather than draw unnecessary attention to himself and this makes him a great actor. The role of any good actor is to get under the skin of the character—Madan Puri was very adept at that.

It is hardly surprising therefore that while some of the biggest stars in Hindi cinema may have acted in say, 100 plus films, Madan Puri was in more than 400 in his 44 years long career—that's an astonishing eight films a year; it shows he was always in demand and directors were keen to include him in the cast, confident that he would bring tremendous value to the film.

This is not the place to list all his films, but some of his more memorable roles deserve attention. The ones that stand out and will be recalled by film buffs, are Yash Chopra's *Waqt*, where, as a gangster, he managed to hold his own in a film full of the big stars of the day. Who does not remember him lurching in a party or trying to pick a fight with Rajkumar? He was also terrific in *Deewar* (also directed by Chopra), as crime boss Samant. Two of his less known but equally well enacted roles were in *Aadmi Aur Insaan* and *Gaddar*, a small but entertaining film that had all the famous (notorious) villains in it. There are many more that come to mind.

But more than any other, I have always thought of Madan Puri as the quintessential Chinaman. In the 1950s, Shakti Samanta, who went on to make soft romantic films such as *Aradhana*, *Kati Patang* and *Amar Prem*, was known as a director of Noir-ish crime films. Samanta was clearly inspired by Hollywood crime dramas, but the tone and mood was distinctly Indian. Two of the best in the series were *Howrah Bridge* and *China Town*, both set in Calcutta. In between there was a third film, the not so well known *Singapore*. Madan Puri played John Wong in the first, Chang in the second and Joseph Wang in the third. A lesser actor would have merely played them all the same way. Not Madan Puri, who brought subtle changes in inflexion and body language to each one of these characters.

Good character actors can switch, chameleon like, into any role. Stars usually play themselves–the audiences don't like their favourites to move too far away from their screen personas. Character actors have more leeway and the better ones, such as Madan Puri, effortlessly take on the persona of whatever role they play. Which is why, Madan Puri, after being a 'villain' for decades, became a kindly grandfather in *Dulhan Wohi Jo Piya Man Bhaye*.

I am happy to note that Madan Puri's son Col Kamlesh Puri has written a book on his father. What is even better is that instead of merely focusing on his film career, the book takes a look at the man behind the actor and gives us a glimpse of what life was like in the 1940s and 1950s, when Madan Puri was settling down in the industry.

One is charmed to read that throughout his life Madan Puri lived in the same small flat he had moved into when he came to Bombay and what is more, sat on his favourite carpet in the centre of the living room, preferring to be with his family rather than spending time in film parties. It reflects his simplicity and domesticity. There are many such vignettes—his struggle to break into the film industry, his early successes, his hey day as a much-in-demand actor—that add to our knowledge about both, the man and the actor. Books on character actors are few and far between—this is a valuable addition to our knowledge about the Hindi film industry.

Sidharth Bhatia
Journalist and Author

# 1 | THE VILLAIN ON THE CARPET

I have tried to portray Madan Puri's life from the unique perspective of a son. My only regret is that I started writing this book more than twenty-five years after his death, by which time many of his colleagues had passed away. Many engaging anecdotes must have gone with them.

My father's film career spanned forty years, from 1945 to 1985. He worked in more than four hundred movies and portrayed every conceivable type of character – hero, villain, comedian, sympathetic, elderly – and each character was unique.

Madan Puri's father, Lala Nihal Chand Puri was born in 1883, four years before Harishchandra Sakharam Bhatavdekar imported a cine-camera from London and filmed the first Indian documentary. Madan Puri was born in 1915, the year in which the Royal Opera House opened its doors in Bombay and also the year in which M K Gandhi returned to India permanently. From then on Indian Cinema and Madan Puri matured together.

From an early age Madan Puri wanted to be an actor. His father encouraged his children to participate in *bhajans* and 'Ram Lila' performances. In addition, Madan Puri's maternal grandfather was a regular performer at the *Harballabh Das ka Mela*. It was in this milieu that Madan Puri, his elder brother Chaman Puri and younger brother Amrish Puri grew up.

Madan Puri's acting career began in 1936, when he performed at the Gaiety Theatre in Simla in *Maal Gaadi*, a play directed by Chaman Puri. Madan Puri was the hero, with Pran playing the female lead. Who was to know that the two amateurs would vie for villainous roles in later years?

In 1944 K L Saigal moved from Calcutta to Bombay. My father was in Calcutta in government service while K L Saigal was there, and often performed small/minuscule roles in his films, which further whetted his appetite for acting. Anticipating better opportunities in Bombay for his cousin, K L Saigal advised Madan Puri to come to Bombay.

In Bombay, Madan Puri was signed on as a hero in five movies. Unfortunately two movies did not do well at the box office, and another producer, Mazhar Khan died of a heart attack before the other three were completed. Work dried up till Dev Anand, who became a close friend, suggested that Madan Puri try his hand at being a villain. He portrayed the villain in *Vidya, Namoona* and *Jeet,* and all three were super hits. He also played the bad guy in V Shantaram's film *Jhanak Jhanak Payal Baje.* His performance as a Chinese in *Howrah Bridge* and in *China Town* made him the stereotype for Chinaman roles.

In *Pyaar Ka Saagar* starring Rajendra Kumar, Meena Kumari and Madan Puri, Meena Kumari married Rajinder Kumar's elder brother Madan Puri in a case of mistaken identity. The movie did not do well because the audience could not accept the heroine marrying anybody but the hero, and the villainous Madan Puri was definitely not acceptable. Dev Anand's *Kala Bazaar* gave him a great opportunity to showcase his talent. However, times changed, and in *Purab Paschim* he played Saira Banu's father and the role was well received. This was followed by *Aradhana* (1970) and *Raftaar.* A spate of positive roles led to a great performance in *Dulhan Wohi Jo Piya Man Bhaye. Noorie* was another great performance. In *Kranti,* Madan Puri's tragicomic performance in a small cameo role was much appreciated by the then Prime Minister Atal Bihari Bajpai at a special screening of the movie.

In 1981 Madan Puri was to visit Jodhpur for the shoot of *Abdullah*. On reaching Delhi he found that all trains were cancelled due to a railway strike. Undeterred, he hired a taxi, travelled through the night and reached in time for the sunrise shoot. His commitment to his work was total – even for dubbing, which he disliked because he said it ruined spontaneity. If he found that his shooting had been called off at the last moment, he would ring up his other producers and offer to come to work if required. As a result he was popular with the producers, and at one point in the seventies had twenty-two movies simultaneously on sets and screens. It was jokingly said that if you wanted to make a movie then all you needed was an Arriflex camera, some raw film and Madan Puri.

My father was a dedicated family man, spending as much time as he could with his wife and children. He was also a devoted grandfather who made it a point to attend every one of his grandchildren's birthdays. For many years he hosted innumerable relatives. Most of his life at home was spent on the living-room carpet, which was office, reception area, dining room and bedroom all in one. I always remember him sitting there in the mornings reading the paper or shaving. Much as he enjoyed acting, my father never entertained the film world at home. He had begun his movie career as a married man with children, and he kept his private and professional lives strictly separate. His children and later, his grandchildren, were not encouraged to attend premieres or other *filmi* events.

Madan Puri's passing was mourned by all, and most studios rescheduled their shootings for a few hours so that everyone could attend his funeral.

I remember being astonished by the size of the crowd. They were all his friends and admirers.

So what was his legacy? More than thirty years after his death Madan Puri is still remembered as a great character actor by his colleagues and by the public. It is said that Indian movies have done more to bring about national integration than all the exhortations of the political, religious and social leaders of the country. I like to think that my father played some part in uniting his country, even as he entertained it.

# 2 | THE FUNERAL

The scene at the Sion crematorium was extraordinary. Hundreds of people had come to pay their last respects to one of Bollywood's most-loved character actors. For the first time I understood that my father had been no ordinary person.

Madan Puri passed away on 13 January 1985, at 1815 hrs. Within minutes, the news was flashed on Doordarshan. They showed vignettes from his movies continuously thereafter. The Minister for Information and Broadcasting expressed his sincere sorrow at the loss of a thespian, and sent a letter of condolence to the family. The news spread fast, and our phone was jammed; callers enquired about the funeral arrangements and paid their respects to the great soul. News reporters rang constantly, asking for details about his illness and death, about the family, and the reaction of the film industry. In Bollywood there was a moment of silence to mourn the passing of a good and popular man.

Early next morning we went to Breach Candy Hospital to bring our father home, and found Pran Saab waiting for us. Pran and Bauji were friends from their amateur theatre days. He escorted Bauji on his final journey, and stayed till the flames had claimed the body. Mourners began to gather below our residence at R P Masani Road from early morning, and TV crews took up vantage positions.

As we brought our father's body into the building I remembered the innumerable times he had carried us up the stairs. Today it was his children who carried him up and tenderly laid him down on the sitting-room carpet.

That carpet had been the only living space that Madan Puri and his wife had been able to save for themselves in the modest, always crowded, two-bedroom flat. He was so hospitable that his guests occupied the bedrooms, while he lived and slept most of his life on the carpet.

The carpet was where he met his producers, directors and studio representatives. Phone calls for shooting dates, confirmations, and cancellations were made from the carpet. It was where he socialized, ate dinner with his family and guests, and played cards with his wife and daughters-in-law. In the morning he would sit on the carpet to shave and read his newspaper, all the while looking onto the lane below and watching the comings and goings. He particularly enjoyed the school children calling out to each other: 'The bus is came!' From his carpet he watched his family come and go. He liked them to dress well but modestly, and if he found something indecorous he would make a gentle remark. We often saw him rehearsing his dialogues or making faces at the mirror, stretching his facial muscles to keep the lines at bay.

In later years, we enjoyed a drink with him in the evening (again on the carpet!) and heard his anecdotes for the nth time. After dinner there was a session of Ludo or Rummy with his wife and daughters-in-law. Then the set would change: sheets would be spread, and the bed was ready. Living on the carpet became such a habit that later, even when my elder brother and his family had moved to a nearby neighbourhood, and my family had joined me in my army posting, Bauji, Beeji, Ramnesh and the family dog still preferred to sleep on the carpet!

The family now gathered around to say their individual goodbyes and remember some cherished moments. Sita Ram Puri's children were there: Sarla aunty and her husband, Col S K Laroiya, and younger sister Varsha. Their brother Purshottam and his wife Veena had rushed from Solan, and their youngest brother Pritam and his wife Prem had come in from Pune. The two families were close: after the early death of Sita Ram chachaji they had all lived under the same roof.

Sneh, widow of Bauji's favorite cousin Inder Kumar Puri of the Railways, was present. Bauji always advised us to emulate I K Puri's maturity, simplicity and straight-forwardness.

Raghuvansh Puri had come from Pune with his wife. He was Bauji's nephew, but they had gone to school and college together. One of the largest poultry farm owners in the country, his speciality was the double-yolked egg, bought by hotel owners for customers who ordered two eggs sunny-side-up.

My maternal uncles, Bhim Sain Vadhera and his wife Savitri, and Mohan Lal Vadhera and his wife Janak, had rushed from Pathankot. My in-laws were present. Pravesh and his wife Veena, his mother-in-law and Veena's two brothers had come to pay their last respects. Ramnesh's in-laws, Col and Mrs P B Singh had rushed from Panna (MP).

Manmohan Krishna helped to oversee the funeral arrangements while Kiki aunty sat with my mother. Our families had known each other since the turn of the last century.

It was time to carry Bauji downstairs to the garden for his last public performance. R P Masani Road residents wept silently as they watched an honoured son taking his last journey. They had seen the young man who had arrived nearly four decades ago with a small family and one trunk become one of their most responsible citizens. As he matured he had won the respect and affection of all the residents of the lane. He had always reached out to anybody who needed help. He accompanied their funeral processions, no matter how busy he was. Should he be out of town when somebody passed away, he would visit as soon as possible for condolences, and offer assistance if required. He was always ready to interact with the authorities if somebody had a problem. The school buses came and went, but now Madan Puri would no longer keep a watchful eye.

The number and variety of people assembled at our residence was astonishing. There were the local officials with whom Bauji had interacted. There were the vegetable vendors; whenever they came, Bauji would teasingly call out to Beeji to come and meet her uncle or aunt. On the day after the cremation one of the long-time sabziwallas tearfully gave my mother some vegetables, but declined to take any money. He said, 'The pleasure of coming to your house was to meet Puri Saab, and this is a humble gift in that memory.' He also said that Saab always bargained hard and then paid them more than the asking price. On Sundays the front door was always left open so that the vegetable vendors and the neighbours could come in to watch *Ramayana* and *Mahabharata*. There were the postmen who had delivered our mail for years and had collected their Diwali *bakshish* from Bauji. A taxi driver told everybody how Madan Puri had one day stopped on a lonely road and allowed the man to siphon out a bottle of petrol, so that he could reach the nearest pump. The driver had stopped plying for the day to attend the funeral. There was the Lane Security Team which Bauji had helped set up many years ago. The eunuchs always stopped at our doorstep during their rounds to indulge in some word play with Bauji and would ask him for money. He would decline, saying, we are professional associates. They too had come to offer condolences. One of Bauji's favourite stories was of the Immigration Officer at Kabul Airport who asked Bauji about his profession. My father replied, '*Pesha-e-kanjar* – a professional entertainer.'

Most of the film *biradari* had arrived at the house to escort Bauji on his last journey.

One of the first to arrive was Sanjeev Kumar, who came from the ICU at Breach Candy with an oxygen cylinder strapped to him. Many people commented on his presence, and he replied, 'A great man has passed away, and I had to come!' Two months later Sanjeev Kumar had joined Bauji in heaven. He was not even fifty.

Sanjiv Kumar was followed by Ashok Kumar. Dharmendra came in after that but he was so heartbroken that he sat inside the bedroom and kept on crying piteously.

Chayya Mehta recorded the list of mourners in Mayapuri No 542/1985. She said, 'I cannot recollect any occasion when any person from the film trade may have passed an adverse comment on Madan Puri. He was not only a hero and a villain and a character actor and a thespian actor but he was a complete gentleman.... I recollect that I was visiting the set of *Kranti*. Madanji had just sat down to have his lunch when Hema Malini and Manoj Kumar came up to say that the next shot was ready, and when Madanji has finished his lunch we shall take the shot. Madanji immediately got up and said, "Shot first, food later!"'

Among the *filmwallahs* who came to bid Madan Puri farewell at our house and at the cremation grounds were Raj Kapoor, Shammi Kapoor, Randhir Kapoor, Rishi Kapoor, Anil Kapoor, Ashok Kumar, Pran, Prem Chopra, Shakti Samantha, Gulshan Nanda, Jeetendra, Vinod Mehra, Dara Singh, K N Singh, Amjad Khan, B R Chopra, Yash Chopra, Dharam Chopra, Ravi Chopra, Manoj Kumar, Ramanand Sagar, Prem Sagar, Anand Sagar, F C Mehra, Umesh Mehra, Rahul Rawail, H S Rawail, Subhash Ghai, N N Sippy, Raj Kumar Kohli, Boney Kapoor, S K Kapoor, Mohan Sehgal, Mushir-Riyaz, Ramesh Behl, Ramesh Talwar, Raj Kishore, Jairaj, Dheeraj, Tej Sapru, Baldev Khosa, Om Prakash, Sharad Saxsena, Jeevan, Suresh Oberoi, Narendra Nath, Asit Sen, Sudesh Kumar, Subiraaj, Dinesh Saxsena, Jugnu, Manohar Deepak, Ghanshyam, Desh Gautam, K D Shorey, Kamal, Gulshan Bawra, Nirmal Anand, Satish Khanna and many other fans, admirers and family members.

Some of the ladies sat with Beeji at home while others went to the cremation grounds. Amongst them was Poonam Dhillon, who said, 'The uniqueness of Madan Puri's personality was such that anybody of any age and any status could sit and have a discussion with him. He was open to all.' Sarika, Dimple Kapadia, Rameshwari, Shammi and Aruna Irani had also come.

Some junior artistes were standing mournfully by as we brought Bauji down, and accompanied us to the cremation grounds. My father had always treated them as colleagues, and sometimes during shooting breaks had shared a cup of tea with them. On one occasion he had forced a senior producer-director-star to apologise to a junior artiste in public after the producer had slapped the junior.

Work stopped on the studio sets for several hours as most of the stars and the staff had come to see off their friend and colleague.

The long procession wound through King's Circle and Matunga. Finally we arrived at the crematorium, where our family *pandit* along with our dear neighbour, Om Bhasin, took over. Om had always been the first to arrive in a crisis, to do whatever was necessary to help the grief-stricken family.

At the cremation grounds, a sea of people moved slowly towards the burning ghat. I looked around at the many familiar faces, Bauji's friends, acquaintances and well-wishers, and realised that my father, in his own quiet and simple way, had become a part of everybody's life. All these people, from the most famous to the simplest common man, had come here to pay him their last respects.

We had often chided Bauji that he was not a recognised figure, despite having worked so long in the movies. He always smiled and said, 'You guys do not know the depth of respect and affection that I enjoy in the industry. Some day you will find out.'

Today, he must have smiled from above as he saw the vast attendance.

Madan Puri shared a great relationship with most of his directors, producers and co-stars. With some it developed into a deep friendship, as with Shakti Samantha. They were close friends much before Shakti Sahib became rich and successful. Shakti Saab accompanied his friend up to the cremation grounds while his wife Neelima stayed back home with Beeji.

Many years later, Manoj Kumar recollected the passing away of my father. He said, 'I am a very God fearing man, but the day

Madan Uncle died, even I questioned why God had to take away such a good man.' Manoj Kumar walked the last mile with Bauji, while his wife sat with my mother. When the smoke started to rise to the western skies, Manoj Kumar said to Raj Saab, 'A good man has gone.' Raj Kapoor, with tears in his eyes, said, 'Madan uncle will always live on.'

Ashok Kumar came to see off his old friend. It was very rarely that he attended a funeral. For Madan Puri he made an exception.

The entire Chopra family was present. The family connections go back more than four decades. Bauji worked in *Waqt* (1965). After that, as Ravi Chopra put it, Madanji was family.

Sunil Dutt Saab could not come to the funeral as he was attending Parliament. On his return, he and Sanjay drove straight from the airport to pay their respects to our mother. Sunil Dutt's bonding with Bauji went back to the days of *Insaan Jaag Utha* (1959).

Shatrughan Sinha was accompanied by his wife Poonam. She had worked with Bauji in *Dharti Ki God Mein*. She remembered Bauji as a very joyous artiste, who was friendly and courteous to all and was especially considerate to the younger stars.

Lekh Tandon had lived and worked in *Punjabi Gully* as part of Prithvi Theatres. He directed *Dhulan Wohi Jo Piya Man Bhaye (DWJPMB)*, which reinforced Madan Puri's image as a character actor.

Rameshwari, the heroine of *DWJPMB* said that the warmth, affection and encouragement that Madanji gave to younger artistes was amazing. Madanji had a great sense of timing and that made him a natural for comedy roles.

Raj Kumar Kohli said, 'The moment Puri Sahib worked in my first movie, he became a family member and from then on he was always in the next movie. Working with him was stress-free. His talent required little guidance.'

Tom Alter told me that one of the people who had influenced his life was Madan Puri. Madanji always generated an aura of inner contentment, he said. He enjoyed his work, was comfortable on the sets and made everybody else feel comfortable. Yet his professionalism was only a shot away.

Kamini Kaushal, who had worked with my father in twelve movies, remembered him as a friend and a very good actor. She said Madanji's passing away left a vacuum. He was very warm hearted and there was no aggressiveness in his work. He never tried to upstage his co-artistes nor was he critical of anybody's performance.

Chaman tayaji was devastated by his brother's death. Born three years apart, they had grown up together. They had met nearly every day at the studios or at home. Chaman tayaji felt he had lost his closest friend.

In his autobiography 'The Art of Life', Amrish chachaji recorded that he got the FilmFare Award for *Meri Jung* (1985) in the same year that his great brother died. He considered it a blessing from his elder brother. He said, 'He loved me from the core of his heart. I have yet to come across such a great actor, a great human being and an affectionate and considerate man. With his departure I have lost a great guardian… He is remembered in our Industry with a lot of reverence… all my adulation for him would always fall short of whatever I might say about him… As a matter of fact, if I have learnt anything in my life as a worldly man, who understands life, I learnt it only from Madan Bhai Saab. He was so meticulous in his approach to everything and he knew how to go about it.'

Harmeet Khaturia, in the magazine *Movies* in February 1985, said that Madan Puri demanded no respect for his seniority and ensured that nobody treated him like an elder. He felt that Madanji's cameo in *Kranti* was the best piece of acting in the film. When he met Madanji on the sets in 1984 and saw him frail and weak, he scolded him, saying, 'You are not well. You should stay at home and not come to work.' Madanji replied, '*Arre Bhai*, sit at home and do what? I'll get bored. It is better to die of illness than to die of boredom.'

We held the Kriya rituals at R P Masani Road. Among those who came to pay a final homage to our father's memory were Shakti

Samantha, the entire B R Chopra Family, N N Sippy, Chandrashekar, Sunil Dutt and Sanjay Dutt, Raj Babbar, Vinod Mehra, Moushami Chatterjee, Kumar Gaurav, S D Burman, Lakmikant, Sonik Omi Anand Bakshi, Vijay Anand and many others

As we performed the final rites, I reflected on the life of a man who overcame all obstacles to achieve his dream to be in the studio with his makeup on, the lights shining and the camera running.

Perhaps, I thought, he had not achieved all his dreams, but then, who has?

*Kisiko mukamal yeh sara jahan na mila*
*Kisiko zameen aur kiskiko asmaan na mila.*

# 3 | BEGINNINGS

Lala Nihal Chand Puri, born in 1883, was fifteenth in the line of Baba Khambewala of Batala district, Gurdaspur. Guru Nanak Devji, the founder of Sikhism and his *baraat* had stayed in our ancestral home in Batala while on their way to Dera Baba Nanak in 1487. Our family continues to enjoy his blessings.

When both his parents and his twelve-year-old wife died of the plague, Nihal Chand Puri left school and got a job in order to look after himself and his younger brother Sita Ram Puri. He then taught himself English. Nihal Chand and his second wife Ved Prakash Kaur, of Nawanshahr, Hoshiarpur, had five children, of whom Chaman Puri (1913–2002), Madan Puri (1915–1985) and Amrish Puri (1932–2005) made names for themselves in the film industry. His daughter Chandra Kanta lives with her husband Rajesh Mehra in New Delhi; their only child Rakesh lives with his family in Australia. The youngest child Harish Puri retired as a Manager with Indian Oil. Harish and his wife Saroj live in Nasik and shuttle between Pune and Delhi, where his two married daughters live, and their son's residence in Texas. When we were children we used to write postcards to our grandfather, Nihal Chand Puri, and he would promptly reply and point out the many grammar and spelling mistakes that we had committed. He always carried a bunch of un-replied letters and blank postcards in his pocket and would pen a reply in his spare moments.

Nihal Chand Puri was a teetotaler and a non-smoker but he was very fond of music and drama. He could neither sing, dance nor act, but he encouraged his children to participate in *ram lila, bhajans, kirtans* and stage plays, and thus, unwittingly, sowed the seeds of his sons' acting careers. Madan's maternal grandfather, who was a good singer and performed regularly at the *Harvallabh Das ka Mela*, might have also influenced Madan and his siblings.

Bade Bauji was in government service in Delhi, and was in charge of the office cash box. His office timings were quite unique. He left home every morning for a walk of ten to fifteen miles. If a colleague had happened to mention that good vegetables or fruit were available at a distant market, our grandfather would go there, deliver some purchases to his daughter's house, take the rest home, and then go to the office, a couple of hours late. However, he was meticulous in his accounts and never left the office till every rupee had been accounted for. Though this tardiness was inherited by some of his children, Madan Puri and Amrish Puri were known for their punctuality.

When they lived in Shimla, Bade Bauji would take Chaman and Madan for an evening walk to the Mall after he returned from office. The Mall in Shimla was the place to see and be seen in the summer. Everybody came out to enjoy the sun and watch the world go by. The brothers dreaded this excursion, for it included Urdu grammar and mathematics. Bade Bauji's walking stick provided the punctuation and the boys provided the exclamation marks. It was no consolation to Chaman and Madan that other children were to be seen on similar happy jaunts!

In those days, employees in the Viceroy's Office maintained a winter home in Delhi and a summer home in Shimla. New Delhi virtually became a ghost town during the summer. It was a great sight to see the Viceroy's entourage and many government offices move out to Shimla by train and bus. The schools moved too, and though the location had changed, the syllabus was the same and the classmates familiar. Madan studied in DAV School in Delhi and Shimla. For the children the move to Shimla was a welcome break and a great adventure. However, Madan Puri actually got to see snow for the first time in his life during the shooting of Shakti Samantha's *Evening in Paris* in 1964.

Madan did not enjoy playing cards unless it was a friendly game with minimal stakes. Behind this aversion was a childhood memory of Shimla. Chaman and Madan and their friends would go down to a place called Tooti Kandi to collect wild walnuts. A friend who was an expert at playing marbles would invariably suggest a game near the base of the hill. Surprisingly, in spite of his expertise, he would lose all his almonds. The other boys would happily carry their winnings up the hill. Near the top, he would again suggest a game of marbles, win everybody's loot and take it all away. It took the boys some time to realize that they were being used as cheap labour!

The freedom struggle was gaining momentum. Chaman and Madan began attending meetings and taking part in processions. Bade Bauji called both his sons and said, 'I am proud of the fact that you are both nationalists. But, I suggest that while you devote yourselves wholeheartedly to it, there are many other ways to serve the motherland, for which you will need to carry on with your studies.'

Madan joined Hindu College, Delhi. They were always at loggerheads with St. Stephen's, whose sophisticates considered the Hindu College boys to be rustics. When they played cricket, the spectators from Hindu College would carry hockey sticks to disrupt the game when they were losing.

During his college days Madan had a good friend in Shimla, Rajinder Krishan, who wrote poetry and recited it to his friends. He went on to gain popularity when he wrote the song *Suno suno aye duniya waalon Bapuji ki amar kahani*. Mohammed Rafi sang it and the music was composed by the brothers Husnlal-Bhagatram. Another great song by him is *Yeh zindagi usiki hai jo kisi ka hogaya* for the movie Anarkali (1953).

Later, Rajinder Krishan moved to Bombay and settled in Pedder Road. His children were about our age and the mothers got along very well. We would be sitting together when Rajinder Krishan uncle would go into his study and emerge after a few minutes to say that he had just penned another song. In the 50's and 60's, Rajinder Krishan was the rage of the South. Nearly every Hindi movie made in Madras had lyrics penned by him.

Bauji used to narrate an anecdote about the time when he was shooting in Madras in the mid-sixties and Rajinder uncle's son was on the same sets as an assistant director. A message was received that the boy should speak to his father on a trunk call from Bombay. Bauji asked him if all was well; he smiled and said that Dad had called to say that he had just won a ₹ 40 lakhs jackpot at the Mahalaxmi Race Course and he wanted his son to come down for a day if possible. Rupees 40 lakhs was a huge amount during the sixties and is very much a considerable sum even today!

1937 was a landmark year for Madan. He graduated from Delhi University with a BA of which he was very proud. By then my grandfather had bought a house in a good mohalla in Pathankot. One day as Madan was walking through the narrow lane of the mohalla, he was observed by the wife of Lala Baij Nath Wadhera, one of the rich and influential men of Pathankot. She liked the look of the boy and after some enquiries decided that he would be her son-in-law. Her husband was surprised because the young man's financial and social status was below theirs, but the lady prevailed.

Despite his objections that he was too young, and not yet settled in life, Madan was married in 1939 to sixteen-year-old Sheela Wadhera. 'The alliance offer was too good to let it pass,' said Bade Bauji.

In those days young people rarely saw their future spouses or their future in-laws before marriage. I once asked Bauji how it was that arranged marriages worked. He jokingly said that after one night together any newly married couple would be friends.

Now that he was married, Madan was adamant that he should find a job so that he could support his family. My grandfather was equally adamant that as a graduate Madan must seek work in keeping with his educational status. Finally, he took a job in Shimla as a teacher. Madan was very fond of dramatics and had performed on stage while in school. In later days he always fondly remembered the time in the thirties, when he was twenty-one and Pran was seventeen, and they acted together in a play *Maal Gaadi* under the direction of Chaman tayaji at the Gaiety Theatre in Shimla.

My mother's maternal home was a four-storied structure with over thirty rooms. Her circumstances changed considerably when she moved to her husband's much smaller home in Shimla. The family included Chaman Puri and his wife, seven-year-old Amrish, the youngest brother Harish and their sister Chandrakanta. The youngsters wanted to spend all their time with their new *bhabhi*, even sleep in her bedroom – a very small storeroom, which had to be vacated early in the morning as it led into the kitchen. So much for the joy of living in joint families! But Beeji never complained. She was as strong-minded as her mother, and nothing daunted her. She had also inherited a sense of personal discipline from her father.

One day, Madan took his bride for a walk in the Mall. As a newly married woman she could not go out unescorted, so Chandrakanta and her cousins Sarla and Varsha went with them. The bride was wearing a heavily embroidered salwar kameez, lots of jewellery and tons of make-up. She was also wearing high heels, which she had never worn before. Her head was covered by a heavy dupatta, which was pulled well over her face so that all that she could see were her own two unsteady feet. The colourful procession wound its way along the Mall with Madan, the proud stud, walking ahead, while my mother and her escorts walked in a tight group behind him. After having done the sights, they wended their way home. In the evening Bade Bauji came home in a blazing temper. He was livid, yelling, 'Madan, you have destroyed my reputation and my standing in society. How could you so brazenly walk around on the Mall

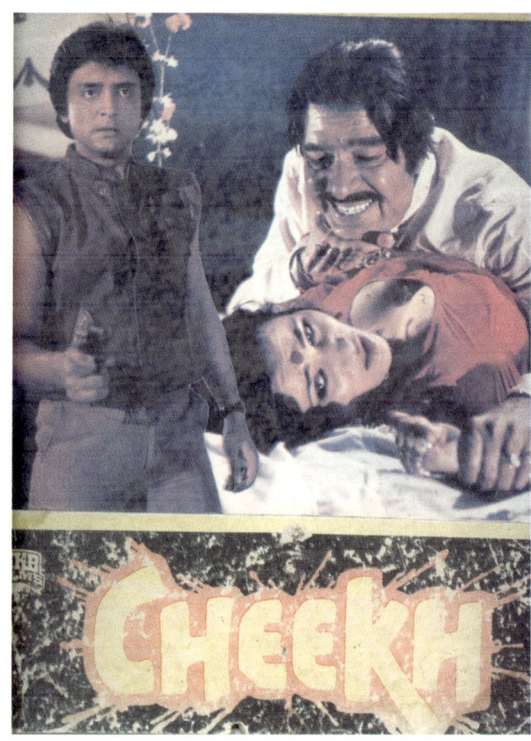

In *Captain Nirmala*

With Javed Khan and Deepika in *Cheekh* (1985)

With Shashi Kapoor in *Mohabbat Isko Kehte Hain* (1965)

With Meena Kumari in *Pyaar Ka Saagar* (1961)

At the inauguration of the Cine Artistes Associaton. The handwritten annotations
were done by Madan Puri.

With Kuldip Kaur and Randhir in *Sheroo* (1957)

With Kesari and Jeevan Kala in *Mr X in Bombay* (1964)

## Lights, Camera, Action!!!

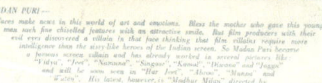

As featured in *Film India* magazine

With Suresh, Suraiya, Sunder and Ravikant in *Goonj* (1952)

In a Punjabi movie with Sunder

With Vijaya Mohini in *Kuldeep* (1946)

With Dev Anand in *Kala Bazaar* (1960)

With Anoop Kumar and
Randhir in *Sheroo* (1957)

With Om Prakash, Kundan and Randhir in *Sheroo* (1957)

With Jaymala and Bela Bose in *Harishchandra Taramati* (1970)

with your wife and your sisters!' That was the end of my mother's romantic honeymoon in Shimla!

Bauji's search for a better job led him to Karachi in 1941, where he worked in the P&T department at the handsome salary of ₹ 90 per month. In 1942 he took a job in Calcutta in the Supply Department of the Director General of Munitions Production. As the war threatened to reach Calcutta, Bauji dispatched his family to Pathankot.

Whilst he was in Calcutta my father had an office colleague with whom he shared bachelor digs, and who was something of a practical joker. One day, he turned up in my father's room with the latest magazines, both Indian and foreign. My father was quite surprised, as they were expensive. The next Sunday, the colleague took my father along for a very early morning walk in one of the posh localities of Calcutta. They walked behind a newspaperman who was making his rounds. Every time the man delivered a newspaper or magazine, the colleague would rush in and pick up a selected magazine.

On another occasion, my father was having dinner with his friend. The dessert was '*rasmalai*'. Whilst they were eating, the friend said, '*Madan, apna ghar samaj ke khao.*' After a few moments the same message was repeated. Dad turned around and said to his friend 'Yaar, don't worry I am comfortable,' and continued eating. The friend said, 'Madan, in your own home you would eat rasmalai with a small spoon but here you are using the large serving spoon.'

By 1944 the threat of war had receded from India, and Bauji moved his family back to Calcutta where he rented a terrace studio on Hazra Road, a nice locality. It was the home of a Punjabi family who had unmarried daughters about as old as Beeji, who was then twenty-three. Beeji would spend the day with the girls, and they would look after Peshi and me, aged four and one. On Sundays and holidays, she packed a lunch box and the family would go to some nearby public park for the day. If Bauji had brought Hindi magazines then Beeji would read to him while the children ran around.

She always said that these were the best years of her life. They had a set routine and she had her husband to herself. Sometimes they walked along the promenades to see the big shops with their exotic displays. However, they never dared to enter, as their monthly income was about three hundred rupees. Years later they revisited Calcutta. Bauji took Beeji back to the same shops and told her, 'Now you can buy what you want!' But the moment of longing had passed.

With Ved Sharma's help Bauji got a small appearance in S D Pancholi's *Khazanchi in 1941*. However, this did not lead to further offers, and his film career in Lahore did not take off. Bauji became restless. The nine-to-five routine of a government job was not how he wished to spend the rest of his life: he still wanted to be a film actor. His cousin, K L Saigal was then a big star with New Theatres in Calcutta. My father sometimes visited him at the studios and stood in for a shot when the opportunity arose, as in *My Sister* (1942). He also appeared in *Omar Khayyam*, which starred K L Saigal and Suraiya.

In 1944, Saigal uncle moved to Bombay. He suggested to Bauji that this was a good time to come to Bombay and seek his fortune in the film world. The exodus from Lahore had already started, and Bombay was to be the new Hindi movie centre. It was cosmopolitan and there was plenty of finance available. War creates millionaires.

A cautious and responsible man, Bauji planned his move meticulously. He applied for six months' leave and sent his family to Pathankot. He promised Beeji that he would try his luck in the film world for six months, and if he did not succeed, he would close the '*filmi*' chapter in his life and return to his government job. Then he wrote a four-page letter to his father explaining why he was taking this major step.

# 4 | THE MOVE TO BOMBAY

Geoffrey Kendal must have had somebody like Madan Puri in mind when he said, 'Being an actor must be the best job in the world. It combines romance, travel, the fun of the lottery, the positive tragedy of failure and the will to overcome it.'

(*The Prithviwallahs* by Shashi Kapoor. pg 24.)

The Calcutta Mail pulled into Victoria Terminus. The year was 1945. The passenger carrying a small steel trunk and bedding was different from the others. In his early thirties, he had chiseled good looks, and was well dressed without being sharp. His walk was confident. He could have been a government official or a visiting successful businessman. Madan Puri had arrived in Bombay to try his luck in this city of dreams, where anything was possible.

Madan Puri found his way to the Great Punjab Hotel in Jer Mahal, a semicircular building located across the road from Metro Cinema. I have always wondered why he selected this particular hotel. A possible answer comes from Bunny Reuben's *Follywood Flashback*. He writes about Prithviraj Kapoor's arrival in Bombay in September 1929. Prithviraj Kapoor had stayed at the Kashmir Hotel, also in Jer Mahal. These two hotels may have been popular haunts for *filmi* aspirants who were high on hopes and low on finance. I met the owner of Great Punjab Hotel while researching this book, and he told me that they were not from Punjab! Perhaps the hotel's name was meant to give confidence to upcountry visitors.

I can imagine the young man standing in the third-floor balcony of the Great Punjab Hotel, looking hopefully at the glitzy marquee lights of Metro Cinema. Commissioned in 1938 and described as one of the world's finest motion picture palaces, it was one of the newest additions to the metropolis of Bombay. Just two buildings away was the Armed Forces Building (AFI), where I have lived with my family from 1989 to 1995.

Bauji only stayed at the Great Punjab Hotel for a couple of days. He then moved to his cousin's home at Shivaji Park for some time. Sunder Lal Puri was the CEO of Filmistan Studio and had also acted in Filmistan movies including *Anand Math* (1952), *Nagin* (1954) and *Anarkali* (1954). S L Puri died young, and his courageous wife brought up their five children single-handed.

K L Saigal introduced Madan Puri to many producers and directors. He was signed up as the lead in Mazhar Khan's *Sona,* co-starring Munnawar Sultana. It did not make as much '*sona*' as expected. His other movies as leading man were *Kuldeep, Imtehaan* with Tasneem, *Phool, Kamal* and *Captain Nirmala* and his heroines were Munnawar Sultana, Vijaya Mohini, Tasneem and Rekha. These movies were not successful either. Mazhar Khan succumbed to a heart attack and his remaining projects were shelved.

Dev Anand had arrived in Bombay a few years earlier. Dev Anand and Madan Puri both belonged to Gurdaspur in Punjab and became good friends. Bauji's career as a hero had stalled. He now signed up as a villain in *Vidya* (1948) starring Dev Anand and Suraiya. For the star pair it was mutual admiration that blossomed into love. Suraiya's grandmother was against the relationship on religious grounds, and besides Suraiya was the family breadwinner. Dev Anand would often sit in his Hillman car below our house discussing his personal problems with Bauji.

*Vidya* was Bauji's first success as a dyed-in-the-wool villain, followed by a great performance in *Jeet* (1949), again with Dev Anand and Suraiya. The third success in a row was *Namoona* (1949) starring Kamini Kaushal, Kishore Sahu and Dev Anand, in which Bauji played the villain's role to perfection. His exploitation of Sulochana's dreadful secret was a delight and took him from the preferred role of hero to that of the villain.

When Madan Puri was a student, Ashok Kumar was his favourite film star. He could never have imagined that some day he would work alongside him. He met Dadamuni for the first time on the sets of Bali's *Raag Rang* (1952). He arrived at the studio worrying how he would face the great star. The scene had a lot of dialogue. At the end of the day's shoot, Ashok Kumar embraced him and said, 'Madan Puri, you are a good actor and you have a great sense of timing.'

Madan Puri considered this as one of the biggest compliments he ever received during his career, since Dadamuni was renowned in the industry for his sense of timing. Bauji said it was always a pleasure and a learning experience to work with him. Some of the movies they worked in together were *Raag Rang* (1952), *Bhagwat Mahima* (1955), *Ek Saal* (1957), *Sheroo* (1957), *Howrah Bridge* (1958), *Nai Rahen* (1959), *Raani Mera Naam* (1972), *Anuraag* (1972), *Bada Kabutar* (1973), *Hifazat* (1973), *Dafaa 302* (1973), *Bhanwar* (1976), *Barood* (1976), *Judaii* (1980), *Dard Ka Rishta* (1982), *Raja Aur Rana* (1984).

At the beginning of his film career Madan Puri was earning more than a thousand rupees a month. This was a small fortune for a clerk who had been earning about three hundred rupees. He went on to act in over four hundred movies in the next forty years, first as a villain, and in later years as a character artiste.

Sometime in 1946 Bauji rented a small room at Bora Bazaar and called his family to Bombay. When he saw us disembarking at Bombay Central, he laughed, and said, 'I have told all my friends that my wife has delayed her arrival to Bombay because my sons are not keeping too well, specially the younger one, and here they are looking healthier than well-fed farm animals!'

We stayed briefly at Bora Bazaar as subtentants in a house that primarily housed a wholesale business for children's shoes. Our bed was made up on a durrie spread on the shop linoleum. One night Beeji heard me moaning in my sleep. When she put on the light she found that a rat had bitten my toe till it bled. My parents were very distressed by this, and the next day Bauji went looking for lodgings in Matunga, an upcoming suburb where many of the film people including K L Saigal had moved.

Bauji rented a ten feet by twelve feet room in a building called Shirin Cottage (now Sethi Niwas) on R P Masani Road, popularly known as Punjabi Galli or Hollywood Lane because of the number of film personalities living there. Soon after arriving in Bombay Beeji developed asthma and spent long and miserable nights crouched over a pillow gasping for breath. Life was difficult for my parents because of my mother's ill health, but they were together, and Bauji was enjoying his chosen career.

Punjabi Galli was to be our home forever after. This is where Bauji put down his roots, lived his wonderful life, and departed with great dignity from this world.

# 5 | FRIENDS AND NEIGHBOURS IN PUNJABI GALLI

Movies used to be made around the clock, though producers preferred to shoot by night. As sound was recorded by sync sound, external noise was much less at night. The crowd of film fans was also less. After a couple of months of living in the Panditjee's house as subtenants, Saigal uncle kindly gave us a two-bedroom flat on rent in his own building Radha Kunj (now called Amar Kunj) in Punjabi Gully. Saigal uncle's mother and my grandfather were cousins.

K L Saigal was an affectionate and kindly man. Every evening he screened his movies on the terrace of the building for family and friends. The men would enjoy their drinks while the ladies sat and chatted and the kids ran around. It was not uncommon to see Bal Thackeray, then a cartoonist, at the Saigal house. Lata Mangeshkar was also a regular visitor. Saigal uncle had two daughters, Neena and Beena; his eldest child, Madan Mohan (Gogi) had a wonderful voice, but died before he could fulfil his potential.

At the time of our move to Punjabi Galli the entire Kapoor family stayed in the Lane: Prithviraj Kapoor with his sons, Raj, Shammi, Shashi and their sister Umi; Prithviraj's father Lala Bisheshwar Nath Kapoor and Prithviraj's two sisters Kailash and Shanta. Bauji worked with Raj, Shammi, Shashi and their cousin Subiraj, then with the next generation, Randhir and Rishi, and also their wives Babita and Neetu.

Prithvi Theatres, established in Bombay in 1944 by Prithvi Raj Kapoor, heralded the renaissance of the Hindustani Theatre Movement in India. He was large hearted and a great man indeed. He usually had hordes of young actors staying with him and with his father. One would always see Papaji's brothers Ram, Amar and Vishi, his sons Shammi and Shashi and his nephews Tiger and Narinder Jetley, with other young men like Sajjan and Lekh Raj Tandon around the place. All of them were hardworking and industrious but any spare time they had they would play lane cricket. Mr Lekh Tandon, whose father was a friend of Papaji from earlier days, was also to be seen with them. Mr Lekh Tandon told me that my father always affectionately called them the Loafer Gang.

The famous German-trained producer/director/writer J K Nanda lived opposite our house. He made great movies like *Singhaar, Parwana, Dhakke ki Malmal* and *Chalaak*. In 1954, in collaboration with Rajinder Singh Bedi, he wrote the script for *Mirza Ghalib*, the first Hindi film to win the President's Gold Medal. In his heyday, one would see a veritable line up of beautiful and glamorous stars like Suraiya, Nargis, Nimmi and Madhubala visiting his house. Great film personalities like D N Madhok, A R Kardar and others also visited him regularly.

Manmohan Krishna lived across the road from us. Manmohan chachaji's father and my grandfather were office colleagues and lifelong friends. Manmohan chachaji was a professor of Physics. His wife Nandini (Kiki aunty) was a MA in History and had taught at Islamia College, Delhi. They would frequently come over after dinner to talk about our shared family connections and the film world. Their discussions about the working conditions of the character actors and the junior artistes eventually led to the formation of the Character Actors Association in 1956.

Manmohan chachaji gave me lessons in Algebra, and a few slaps were part of the teaching process. In those days getting occasional slaps was no big deal, and there were no psychological scars or trauma. Our elders loved us and their punishments carried no sting. I was singularly fortunate that I had plenty of loving elders.

Manmohan Krishna won the Filmfare Best Supporting Actor Award for *Dhool ka Phool* and subsequently directed the highly acclaimed Yash Chopra's *Noori*. Bauji played Poonam Dhillon's father in the movie, a positive role superbly played.

Trilok Kapoor lived next door to Manmohan Krishna. He had played Lord Shiva in so many movies that calendars and religious photos depicted him as such. His elder brother Prithvi Papaji often told him jokingly, 'I dare not scold you because you might point your angry Third Eye toward me!'

Jagdish Sethi, a great producer-director-actor who made many classics such as *Jaggu*, lived in the next building. He had acted in *Alam Ara* (1931), the first Indian talkie movie. Jagdish Sethi was also an astrologer who was not afraid of making negative predictions. His son Omesh was my classmate and best friend and we had shared many childhood escapades. Once, Sethi uncle fell seriously ill. Half-joking, Bauji asked him, '*Papaji*, you are always predicting people's future; today, what about you?'

Sethi uncle replied, 'Madan, I am not sure about my exact date and time of birth so my predictions about myself may not be accurate, but I know that Omi's father cannot die as yet.'

He recovered, and lived for many years. Unfortunately Omesh, who rose to the rank of Master Mariner in the Merchant Navy, died of cardiac arrest in 1993, aged barely fifty.

On one occasion, Mohinder Lal Saigal (younger brother of K L Saigal), who lived next door to J K Nanda, took very ill and was admitted to Sion Hospital. One night at about 3 am, Savita, daughter of Jagdish Sethi woke up and saw the light was on in Sethi Saab's room. She walked in and found her father fully dressed and sitting at his table. He said that he was waiting for the phone to ring. A few minutes later, the phone rang. Amrish chachaji, who was on hospital duty that night, informed Sethi Saab that M L Saigal had passed away. Sethi Saheb got up from his table and said that he was going down to the Lane to inform everybody.

Mithun Chakravarty lived for a short period in the back lane in the building next to K N Singh. Jayant, Anil Biswas, Ashalata, Jairaj, Phani Mazumdar, Bismil Peshawari, P N Arora, Sitara Devi and Manna Dey all lived in Punjabi Galli during that period. Dwarka Khosla and Raj Khosla lived nearby. Film producer Dr Sinha and his niece Vidya Sinha, Kanhaiya Lal and Bharat Kapoor also lived in the vicinity. Mr Kakkar, the studio manager of R K Studio, occupied the flat above us. Mrs Kailash Kakkar was Prithviraj Kapoor's sister. Their son Subiraj worked in many movies as the male lead and later worked in TV serials. He married Baby Naaz of '*Boot Polish*' fame – a Raj Kapoor classic. Subiraj and Naaz starred in *Dekha Pyar Tumhara (1963)* and Bauji played the villain. Subiraj passed away in July 2007. Naaz had died some years earlier.

Everybody in the lane got together to celebrate festivals, especially Holi and Diwali. After he moved to Chembur, Raj Kapoor came to his parents' home for their blessings on Diwali for many years, bringing a huge basket of fireworks. All the families came down to watch his Diwali gift to his parents and the lane. Mrs Krishna Kapoor, one of the most graceful and beautiful women in the world, always came dressed in white. On every occasion she would go and touch the feet of all the elders of the lane and seek their blessings. Even today her grace and dignity is incomparable.

The mid-fifties saw an exodus of the film fraternity from Matunga towards Pali Hill, Bandra, where large independent bungalows and spacious flats were available. Now only three film families live in Hollywood Lane: Mrs Manmohan Krishna and her son and family; J K Nanda's widowed daughter-in-law and her daughters; and my younger brother Ramnesh and his children. However, the legendary aura of Hollywood Lane aka Punjabi Galli lingers on.

# 6 | CHILDHOOD IN PUNJABI GALLI

When at home, Bauji's favourite place was the carpet in the sitting room. On one occasion he was sitting by the window shaving, and watching people passing in the street, when he noticed a stranger walking away holding the hand of five-year-old Neetu, daughter of Prithviraj Kapoor's sister, Shanta Dhawan. Suspicious, Bauji called out to him to stop, but the man walked faster. Bauji ran down to the road in his lungi with shaving cream all over his face. The man ran away, leaving the child, and calamity was averted. Bauji never mentioned this incident to us, but home security was tightened. Shanta aunty's son Ricky told me this story in October 2011.

I finally got my first experience of acting in a movie in 1951. Jagdish Sethi was producing the movie *Jaggu*. There was a scene where child artiste Baby Nanda conducts the wedding of her doll. Sethi uncle collected about twenty of the lane's children and put them into the scene. I played the pandit and a friend Dinyar Dubash played the barber. It was a great experience and we were treated to a sumptuous lunch. Sadly my film career did not progress further till many decades later.

Beeji's brother, Bhim Sain, was a member of the Jan Sangh and was often jailed for his political activities. Bauji would tease Beeji, saying, 'Actually your brother must be behind bars for criminal activities.' Hoping that his political activities might lessen, Bauji persuaded my uncle to come to Bombay. Bhim mamaji worked as an electrical engineer in Filmistan Studio for a couple of years. He was unhappy about his political inactivity and embarrassed that he stayed in his sister's house. He returned to Pathankot and combined business and Netagiri.

A few years later, the family was worried about Beeji's younger brother, Mohan Lal, who was apparently sowing his wild oats in Pathankot. Beeji would cry and worry about him so Bauji brought Mohan Lal to Bombay and got him a job. Mohan Lal was petrified of Bauji. Beeji told us why. Bauji had visited his in-laws' home after his marriage for a meal. They placed young Mohan Lal in Bauji's lap to eat with his Jeejaji. The child put his hand into Bauji's plate and started messing around. Bauji hated anybody sharing his plate and quietly encouraged Mohan Lal to bite into a green chilli! He got the message and never forgot it either.

Punjabi Galli was one big family. Shashi Kapoor and my elder brother Peshi were classmates at the Don Bosco High School and played for the school cricket team. Farokh Engineer was the Captain. Lane cricket was a favourite pastime on Sundays and holidays, played right below our house with a fire hydrant as the wicket and a lamp post at the bowling end.

One day Peshi and Shashi got into an argument while playing, and strong words like 'bastard' were exchanged. Bauji was watching from the balcony and felt it was time to salvage the honour of both families. He called out, asking Shashi whether he knew the meaning of the word bastard; Shashi said no, and my brother also feigned ignorance. Bauji told Shashi to go ask his father, called Peshi home, and gave him a 'bastardly' beating. Both the fathers met in the evening and had a good laugh; the boys went to school the next morning as usual. A few years later Shashi was playing the hero and beating up my father, and each was calling the other 'haramzada' –

bastard – and getting paid for it! Bauji laughingly recounted this story to everybody.

Sometime in 1950, Shashi staged a play on his terrace (he stood on a stool and gave a monologue) and charged us children two annas each. Another time he bought a still camera to make a movie. My elder brother and I were offered starring roles – in fact, I suspect that all those who agreed to finance the movie were offered starring roles. On the day of the shooting Peshi and I scrubbed our faces with Lux soap (*Sitaron ki pasand!*) and got ready. Bauji saw us leaving the house, neatly dressed, and his suspicions were aroused.

'Where are you guys going?' he asked.

Peshi said that we were going for shooting. Bauji's withering look would have reduced most mortals to ashes.

'Get back into the house, *ullu ke pathe*. Film career indeed!' said my father.

Bauji had sensed competition, and nipped it in the bud.

Shashi's opening remark when I met him at Janaki Kutir, (his home in Juhu) in 2012 was, 'Thank you for being punctual. I hate people being late. It shows disrespect.'

He is as friendly as in the old days. His smile still lights up an entire room. Shashi said that Madan uncle made it very clear that on the sets they were colleagues and that personal relations, age or social standings, should not be allowed to interfere in their work.

Madan Puri and Shashi worked together in twenty-four movies: *Mohabbat Isko Kahte Hain* (1965), *Waqt* (1965), *Aamne Saamne* (1967), *Juaari* (1968), *Pyaar Ka Mausam* (1969), *My Love* (1970), *Jaanwar aur Insaan* (1972), *Chor Machaye Shor* (1974), *Roti, Kapda aur Makaan* (1974), *Deewar* (1975), *Aap Beeti* (1976), *Fakira* (1976), *Deewangee* (1976), *Chakkar Pe Chakkar* (1977), *Heeralal Pannalal* (1978), *Aahuti* (1978), *Gautam Govinda* (1978), *Tere Pyaar Mein* (1979), *Kaala Pathar* (1979), *Swayamvar* (1980), *Kraanti* (1981), *Sawaal* (1982), *Yaadon Ki Zanjeer* (1984), *Bepanaah* (1985).

On 23 March 2015, the GOI announced that the Dada Saheb Phalke award had been bestowed on Shashi Kapoor for his contribution to the film world and theatre. This award follows the earlier awards given to his father, Prithvi Raj Kapoor, and his brother Raj Kapoor. It is a fitting honour.

There was great solidarity amongst the 'Galli-wallas'. Prithvi Papaji reminded me of an incident while he was walking beside the horse in my *baraat*. When I was about nine I went with a friend to visit his married sister in Parel. I returned home very late, about 10 pm, to find great consternation in the lane. The police were searching the bushes and gardens in all the buildings. All the men, including Prithviraj Kapoor, J K Nanda, Jagdish Sethi, K N Singh and one Mr Dubash – all huge men – had joined in the search. When I entered the Lane I wondered what the commotion was all about. Prithvi Papaji caught me by the scruff of my neck and marched me up to my father. Bauji did not say a word, but took me home. All the ladies were sitting with Beeji, trying to console her. The word spread that I had been found and all was well. The neighbours dispersed. When Beeji saw me, she started sobbing, then, with tears still in her eyes, she gave me the thrashing of my life.

I must have been about ten when Beeji asked me one evening to post a letter in the letterbox in the lane behind our house, about a hundred yards from home. The first *dak* clearance was at 0700 for same day delivery in Delhi. I was reluctant to go, as there was a so-called 'Bhoot Bangla' right opposite the letterbox. It was a beautiful two-storied corner house with a clock above the entrance. The dial sometimes lit up, but the clock never worked. We invented lurid stories about the occupants of the house, the wildest being that there was a beautiful woman imprisoned in a room behind the clock by her family because she was in love with some unacceptable chap. In our fantasies she sometimes escaped at night and strangled people. As a result we avoided going there after dark – and here was my own mother asking me to go there late in the night! After a lot of argument Beeji agreed that I could go first thing in the morning. However Bauji had heard the discussion and acted in a most villainous manner: he told me to go and post the letter NOW!

My father was more to be feared than any fantasy. I took the letter and walked to the end of the lane. I now had to turn the corner, walk fifty yards, go past the *Bhoot Bangla*, cross the road, drop the letter in the letterbox, turn back, and come home. Beeji had taught us that in moments of stress or fear we should recite the Gayatri Mantra and God would protect us. I took a deep breath, started reciting the Gayatri Mantra and ran like hell to the letterbox, dropped the letter into the box and ran back to the safety of my lane. Many world track records were surely broken. My fervent prayers must have woken up all eighty-four lakh Hindu Gods, and a few more. As I turned the corner, I bumped into somebody and stopped short, terrified. It was Bauji. After Beeji had explained the reason for my reluctance to go he had followed me. He and Beeji were always there for us in times of stress.

Ours was a typical conservative middle class home, and during our childhood we saw little affluence. The early years of Bauji's film career were difficult and success eluded him for a long time. He worked very long hours and would often return late in the evening when we had gone to sleep. There was great disparity between his income and fame and that of the top stars like Dilip Kumar, Dev Anand or Raj Kapoor. Once I asked Bauji about this, and he said that the popularity he enjoyed was dependent upon public demand for the actor and had little to do with the actor's ability. He said he was content with what he earned, and his greatest happiness was that he was doing what he wanted to do.

Every year we accompanied our mother to Pathankot during our school vacations. We mostly traveled by Frontier Mail, third class, unreserved. The coolies occupied the train before it left the Yard and you had to bargain with them for seats. At Bombay Central at least two hundred people got into the compartment meant for sixty-five.

This included passengers, their relatives, coolies, touts, pickpockets, baggage stealers, voyeurs and bottom pinchers. The passengers fought with each other for space. I remember once Bade Bauji was travelling back to Delhi with many relatives. The coolie banged a trunk into him and there was BLOOD! The entire Puri khandan including the Chaman-Madan-Amrish trio pasted the life out of the coolie.

Once the train left Bombay Central, the compartment was suddenly two-thirds empty, and safer, as most of the bottom-pinchers and thieves had dismounted to see off another group of passengers, which self-imposed duty they carried out most assiduously. By the time the train reached Dahanu, the passengers had stopped fighting and were busy buying chikkoos. Ratlam saw the passengers making friends with each other and looking around for khoya, and by the time the train reached Kota Jn, we were eating delicious spicy kachoris, exchanging addresses and inviting each other for family events.

My maternal grandfather, who was a prominent citizen of Pathankot, always received us at the station. He got so excited about our arrival that he would sit at the front of the tonga announcing to all and sundry, 'Sheela and the boys have come.' My maternal grandmother (Pabiji) Prakash Kaur received us with unbounded love and affection.

Beeji's maternal home held great interest for us. There was one particular room in which my mother and her three brothers were born. My elder brother Pravesh (Peshi) was born in the same room on 13 April 1940. My second brother Billa was born there in 1942. Unfortunately he died a year later of an undiagnosed illness. I was born in the same room on 9 May 1943. However, Ramnesh (Bobli) was born in Bombay on 13 August 1950. Beeji would walk through the house and proudly show us the large rooms on the ground floor, filled with lagaan brought by the tenant farmers – an abundance of grain, cereals and fruits.

My grandmother was the matriarch of the neighbourhood. Early afternoon, all the women from the *mohalla* would congregate at our house with their little ones and their knitting, and sit and gossip for a couple of hours, or discuss their problems. Most of the women had babies in their arms, in their bellies, or on their minds. If a little one cried and the mother was not around, the nearest woman would pick up the child and latch it on. All the kids of the neighbourhood were milk-related!

The locals were awed that Baij Nathji's English-speaking grandsons were from 'Bumbae', and that our father was a film actor. In fact he was practically considered the town's son-in-law. It was too much for them to digest, and they came again and again to stare at us.

Being the town's son-in-law had its drawbacks. One day the doorbell rang at Matunga, and a young man walked in holding a small trunk. He smelled and looked as if he had just got off a train. My father was sitting on the carpet, shaving. The young man asked for his sister! Enquiries revealed that he ironed clothes below my mother's house in Pathankot, and therefore she was his country cousin. After receiving the mandatory cup of tea he asked where he should put his baggage. He also requested a bath. Dad could be patient, and he asked the young man what had brought him to Bombay. 'I have come to join the films,' said our visitor. When asked what aspect of film making interested him, he said, 'I can do any role – if you wish, I could be the hero!' He was allowed to use the bathroom, and then my father dropped him off at Bombay Central, gave him money to buy a ticket back to Pathankot, and bade him goodbye.

In 1954 our mother went to Pathankot to care for her ailing father. We had no servant, but Bauji was convinced that he and his sons would be able to manage. He made a menu and told Peshi and me to do the cooking, saying that even uneducated village boys and girls could cook, so we should have no problem. One day Bauji bought some karela and as he left for work he told Peshi, 'Today you can make karela, and we shall have them for lunch.' Neither of us had the slightest clue how to cook them. We tried various combinations of putting oil and water and peeling the top off, and were left with about 25 grams of an inedible black mass. Bauji made no comment, but rang up Beeji and suggested that she return soon. However, he was very supportive of our effort.

Bauji loved dabbling in the kitchen; he would come and stir the dal, and then stand on the balcony and inform everybody that he had cooked all the food.

I have always been very inquisitive. Once, while Beeji was away in Pathankot, Bauji was at home and wanted to rehearse his dialogues without any distractions. He closed the door between the sitting room and the next room. Curious, I brought a stool to try and look through the ventilator above the door. Peshi pleaded with me that Bauji would be very angry if I spied on him. Bauji must have heard our discussion because suddenly the door opened, and there I was standing on the stool. He was very angry that I had disobeyed, and a terrific beating followed.

I was barely twelve when Bauji discovered that I had started smoking. He called me to the sitting room. I was prepared for the mother of all beatings, but to my amazement he sat me down and said, 'Look, I have learnt that you have started smoking. I am not in a position to scold you since I am a smoker. However, I feel that you are too young to smoke and besides I think that a man should develop vices (if he has to!) only when he can afford them. Now you may go and do what you think is right.' This was the first time in my life that I had not been given a thrashing for my sins; I had actually been treated like an adult and allowed to make a choice. I did not smoke again for many years till I could afford it.

One day I had a fight with a boy of my age, in the lane just below our house. The boy's father came on the scene and restrained me while his son beat me up. Bauji had been watching us slugging it out from his seat on the balcony. Now he came down and scolded the father for unfairly interfering in a fight between children. When I was leaving, I turned and told the parent, 'I will see you.' Bauji, very upset that I had spoken rudely to an elder, gave me a thrashing when we got home. It was one more lesson to be learned: one should not be rude to elders.

V Shantaram had arranged a week-long musical extravaganza at the Liberty Cinema to celebrate the Golden Jubilee of *Jhanak Jhanak Payal Baaje*. He invited the masters of Indian classical music to come and play for one evening each. Peshi and I complained that we were missing all the fun, so we were kitted out in new clothes and taken to the Liberty Cinema, where Ustad Bismillah Khan on the *shehnai* kept the cognoscenti in raptures for over three hours. We also enjoyed it, but at the age of twelve it was a heavy dose of culture for non-musical youngsters, and besides, the AC was on full blast. After that freezing evening we did not complain. Our mother, no more musically inclined than we were, sat stoically through all the evenings.

Bauji was very particular about answering the phone when he was at home. There were many calls from his fans and admirers, including young ladies. One day my brothers called him from the second phone in the inner room, pretending to be his fans. He answered all their questions about his new movies, and other personal questions. They then requested that he sing for them. Bauji said that he did not know how to sing, which was true. When they insisted, he cleared his throat and started singing. The brothers started laughing and the game was up. Bauji was furious, but he also saw the humour in the situation.

Saigal uncle's son Gogi was addicted to alcohol, the cause of his early demise. One morning he asked me to accompany him to King's Circle. We entered a building and went to the first floor to a bar, where a few men were sitting. This was my first and only experience of visiting a country bar, but I forgot about it until Bauji came home in the evening. He changed his clothes, then asked my mother for an empty glass. He fetched a bottle of whisky from his cupboard, and sat on the carpet. The whole family watched this strange behaviour in petrified silence. He opened the bottle and called to me to come closer and have a drink. Me! Why me? I could not understand why, but his stern look made me cry. He said, you are too young to drink but if you must, then do so at home and not at some miserable Aunty's bar. The message had reached him at the studios that his younger son had visited Michael's Bar. I explained I had only accompanied Gogi and that I had not touched any alcohol. As a result, I did not drink at all till after I became an officer.

# 7 | COMING OF AGE

In 1959 I joined Khalsa College, located near our house. Life was fun. I spent a year in the college and indulged my love for dramatics. The first time I appeared on stage, the College Dramatic Society invited Bauji as the Chief Guest and Manmohan chachaji as the Guest of Honour. The wives accompanied the two gentlemen. I had a very small part, but I was sure that I would dazzle the audience. I walked onto the stage on cue. I looked out at the audience and saw my parents and elders, and froze. I remained frozen for aeons. The next morning, Bauji spoke to me very gently and sympathetically and advised me to select another vocation, as the stage was not for me.

In 1960 I applied for admission to the National Defence Academy at Khadakvasla. One day when I came home from college, Bauji was sitting on the carpet, shaving. He offered to take me to the studios for 'Time Pass'. I immediately sensed that my NDA call must have come, because all these years he had never allowed any of us near the film world. We went to Shree Sound Studios at Dadar. Bauji had no shooting on that day; I suspect he had come just to show me off. We went to one of the sets where Madhubala was shooting. Bauji left me in her care and went off to meet somebody. Madhubala was lying on a bed, rehearsing a scene. During the break in shooting she said, '*Aao beta, aap bhi idhar aakar baith jao.*' I was so totally mesmerized by her beauty that I blurted out,'*Jee, main nahin bethoonga, kyon ki aapne beta kaha.*'

She laughed in her captivating way and narrated the conversation to Bauji on his return, saying, 'Madanji, you are great but your son is way ahead.' Bauji was not amused and announced very loudly that henceforth he would not take me to any film studio.

Bauji watched me lovingly but impatiently whenever I came home on leave. I would spend the whole day lying on the carpet reading paperbacks or listening to *Vividh Bharati*. After lunch I took a siesta, and in the evening I visited my girlfriend Asha. He could not understand why an able-bodied man wanted to be on leave for two months at a time, and would nudge me with his foot and say, 'A man who has not worked during the day has no right to a meal in the evening.'

A great film personality living near our house was Sardar Rajinder Singh Bedi, the noted writer. His acclaimed book *Ek Chadaar Maili Si* has been made into a movie. His son, Narinder Bedi made some great movies in which my father also acted (*Benaam*, 1974, and *Rafoo Chakkar*, 1975).

In 1961, I was returning home late in a taxi, after spending the evening with my wife-to-be. It was raining very heavily and we got stuck in a massive traffic jam on Tilak Bridge at Dadar. I paid off the taxi and started walking homeward. The taxi driver abused all seventeen generations of my family, because he was left in the middle of the traffic and now the meter was not running. I could not give a damn as I was young, madly in love and full of health and vitality due to the good food of the National Defence Academy (3500 calories per day being wasted on useless cadets like you, the Drill Instructor always said).

At many places near Khodadad Circle one could see cars stranded as the water was waist deep and had entered the carburetor. I would give a small push to the stalled cars and carry on walking homewards. Inside one stranded car I saw Rajinder Singh uncle sitting, with the rain pelting away. I commandeered a couple of the opportunistic chokras who are always around to push your car some small distance for large monies. Uncle was half asleep; the late hour and the incessant rain had left him reconciled to spending the night in his car. I paid my respects and introduced myself. He was very affectionate and said, 'Why don't you come inside the car; you are getting wet!'

(He and his car were already hopelessly wet.)

We finally got his car started and then he put his hand into his pocket and produced a wad of notes, which the chokras pounced upon. I grabbed the money from Rajinder Singh Saheb's hand and gave the boys some amount and we drove up to my house, at which point the car stalled again. It was already past 2 am. My house lights were on and Bauji was pacing in the balcony. I took uncle home and used him as the shield for my late coming. My father then drove uncle to his house, which was about a kilometer away. The next day uncle came to collect his car and was very thankful to me.

On another occasion I was on leave and Bauji took me to Shree Sound Studio and introduced me to Dara Singh Saab while he went off to meet some people. During a break in the shooting the staff brought a plate with a dozen boiled eggs cut in halves. Dara Singh invited me to join him, which I did with gusto. When Bauji returned, Dara Singh said, 'Puri Saab, I am 280 lbs and a World Champion. We shared a plate of boiled eggs. I had six and this young soldier had six. My eggs are on my body but where did the six eggs go that this 62 kg young man ate?'

After the Sino–Indian War of 1962 the film industry took out a procession through Bombay to collect money for the National Defence Fund, and the contribution was generous. That evening Bauji returned home very late. He called before leaving Famous Studios at Mahalaxmi saying, somewhat cryptically, that he was carrying a large amount of money and we should help him to bring it up when he reached home. We understood when we went down to the car: he had brought home a couple of thousands in small coins, which had been thrown onto the trucks carrying the stars. It weighed quite a lot! We piled it up on the carpet and ran our hands through it; more money than we had ever seen before! I don't think we slept that night. We were most relieved when Bauji took it to the bank the next morning.

It was not the practice to serve drinks at home. In our childhood, if Bauji ever consumed liquor he would sit in the park near our house and only returned home after we had gone to sleep, so that his sons might never smell alcohol on him. This continued till my elder brother and I became professionals in our own fields. I had my first-ever drink with Bauji in 1964 when I was over 21. I was attending a commando course at the Infantry School, Mhow (MP). My parents and brothers had driven up to see me, as I had come down from Arunanchal Pradesh and was not certain if I would get leave after the course. Like death and taxes, one thing was certain in the Indian Army; young officers never got leave when they asked for it.

After I was done we visited Indore and Ujjain. Om Prakash's younger brother had opened a restaurant called LANTERN in Indore. In a bold move Bauji ordered a bottle of beer, and after a short lecture on the evils of drinking, he split the bottle three ways. This was prompted by the fact that the previous evening while I was out on my final endurance test, Umang Seth, an NDA batch-mate, had hosted my family and served them drinks. Peshi was an officer in the Merchant Navy, and had already visited half the ports in the world and sampled their wares. I was a trained commando – and here was Bauji giving us half a glass of beer each along with a moral lecture! My brother and I looked at each other, and we simultaneously picked up our glasses and finished them in one gulp. Bauji did not think it at all funny and it was with great difficulty that we got him to order one more bottle.

On an earlier occasion Bauji was shooting in Madras and he learnt that Peshi's ship was in port. Bauji went to the docks and located the ship. He was informed that Peshi had gone to the Company Office but would be back shortly. The crew invited Bauji to wait in his cabin.

Bauji found cigarettes on the table, and bottles of beer and whisky. He was quite amused to see sexy pinups adorning the cabin walls. Peshi came in a few minutes later and very confidently offered Bauji a drink. When Bauji asked him about the pinups, Peshi replied that he was a sailor and they amused themselves by looking at these snaps during the long voyages. And here was Bauji offering us a one third portion each of a bottle of beer!

Sometimes old traditions create complications in modern living. Bauji never smoked in front of his father, and drinking with our grandfather was out of the question as he was a teetotaller. The result was that we could drink with our father but smoking was not done. My grandfather stayed with us during my wedding in 1966. Bauji used to go out of the house by the back door to smoke out of sight of his father, while I would go downstairs and stand behind the building wall to smoke out of sight of my father, and Peshi would go and stand behind another wall for the same reason. Anybody taking an aerial view would see a scene ripe for a comedy show.

Bauji was a very emotional and affectionate man, yet I cannot recollect him hugging or kissing us when we were children. He had been brought up in the old style when children were not openly shown affection in case they got spoilt. Once, when I was about seventeen, I came on leave from NDA, and he tried to hug me. When I said that it was rather late in life to show affection, he quietly moved away. Later on Beeji scolded me and said, 'Your father always hugged you two brothers, but only after you had gone to sleep at night.' Ramnesh was luckier. By the time he grew up, customs had changed and Bauji had mellowed.

For our family, our life was a secure world. For that we are grateful to our parents, and we try to ensure that good family traditions are maintained.

# 8 | THE COMMANDO GETS ENGAGED

At the National Defence Academy, Kharakvasla, we have a beautiful auditorium that seats over 2000 people. I did my military training there from June 1960 to May 1963. It soon became known that I was the son of the infamous screen villain, Madan Puri. Whenever there was a movie of my father's, my course mates would call for me in the hall. At the end of the movie, our seniors would dole out punishments to us for having created a ruckus. We invariably had to pick up our cycles above our heads and frog march to the Cadets' Mess for dinner. My friends still call me 'Wong' after Bauji's role in *Howrah Bridge*. I had better luck on the stage at NDA. I participated regularly in dramatics and was a reasonably successful performer. Whenever people met me as an army officer and then learnt that I was a film actor's son, they would be amazed and disbelieving. At one social event, one lady asked me in an incredulous tone 'Your father... your *real* father!!!' That finished my social standing at that event.

During my NDA stint my girlfriend Asha and I met once a month. Asha studied at Jai Hind College and later at Government Law College. Twice a year I got six weeks leave. I would hang around her college premises, much to the annoyance of the local studs who did not dare take on the lean, mean and menacing *mucchi-wala*. My parents had been concerned about me for some time. Whenever I came home on leave I would spend the whole day at home, but would spruce up in the evenings, go out, and return by 10 pm, late by our family standards.

Once my parents decided to have me investigated. One Sunday morning I informed Beeji that I was going to Metro Cinema to attend a movie at the Metro Cub Club. Bauji knew that I was not a member of the Club. He also noted that I had taken great pains to get ready, which was not my normal practice. Amrish chachaji was directed to follow me and do *jasoosi*. I left the house and he left the house. I walked to Matunga Station and he walked to Matunga Station. I caught a train to Marine Lines and he caught a train to Marine Lines. By this time I had spotted him. I reached Metro, and Asha and I disappeared inside the hall. Amrish chachaji was stopped from entering because the show was only for sixteen years and below. The movies at the Metro Cub Club in those days were screened for those below sixteen. I was three months short of seventeen then. Since we did not have a phone at home, Amrish chachaji rang Kiki aunty (Mrs Manmohan Krishna) to tell my father that he had lost contact and had not even seen the girl. Kiki aunty gave him some choice words and told him to come home.

NDA was followed by a year at the Indian Military Academy, Dehradun. On 9 February 1964, I was commissioned as a Second Lieutenant in the Infantry and was raring to get married. However, the Army disapproved of officers marrying before the age of twenty-five because young officers should first learn their profession before they took on the responsibilities of married life. I was only twenty-one.

Asha was also twenty-one and had been introduced to several boys, but she kept putting off the proposals, saying that she wanted to study further. Her younger sister Usha had found a good match and the family did not want to wait indefinitely for her elder sister to tie the knot.

I decided to meet Asha's parents and explain to them that as per Army Rules I could not get married till I was twenty-five. The sisters' father had passed away when they were very young, and thereafter their chachaji, Advocate Bhagwan Das Kundnani, was their father. Accordingly, I met her Chachaji at his house in Sion. Asha's entire family was present to see this Punjabi. I never knew she had so many pretty cousin sisters! To bolster my courage I carried a pipe, which I stuck in my mouth most of the time. The meeting started off well. Mr Kundnani served me a drink, and another, and then a third.

I felt relaxed, and then suddenly the Advocate sprang at me and said, 'What are your intentions?'

The trained commando was not at all flustered by this unexpected attack. My brief reply (through the pipe) was, 'To marry your daughter.'

He countered, 'Suppose I do not agree?'

'We are both adults and you cannot stop us,' I said, gripping the pipe firmly between my teeth. 'I am from a respectable family and in a respectable profession. We shall go away and get married and you will have lost a daughter and a son-in-law.'

Daddy was impressed by this defiant response, but the arguments were not yet concluded. He demanded a meeting with my parents. I had to make similar representations to them before they agreed to meet Asha's parents. Again, the meeting took place at Sion, with all the Kundnanis present as well as the Mirchandanis (my mother-in-law's family). My parents finally got to see the girl who had kept their son enthralled for the past five years. The meeting was good and the families liked each other. My parents fell in love with Asha and her lovely long tresses. The two fathers decided that they would go with our proposed union but that we should wait till I moved to a family station. I was then posted to NEFA (North Eastern Frontier Agency), now called Arunanchal Pradesh. Asha and I agreed to wait.

In 1966, my Unit was scheduled to move to Meerut, a family station. We decided to get married, and our parents agreed. My Colonel most villainously threatened to stop my leave to get married, because I was only twenty-three. I insisted that I had to go. Seeing my determination, he reluctantly agreed. The family pandit was another character. He said a star had crashed that month so no weddings were possible for another year. I had to cajole him with a hundred-rupee note, accompanied by threats of Army Action. He finally said that 23 October 1966, was an auspicious day because it was Dussehra. I reached Bombay by 15 October and started the hectic process of getting clothes stitched, wedding cards designed, catering, and all the millions of things that make an Indian wedding so unique. Asha and I met every day to exchange notes about the craziness surrounding us. Somebody came up with the notion that a formal engagement was absolutely essential, even though we had known each other for six years, our parents had already met, and Asha had been visiting my home regularly for the past two years. No Sir, an engagement was a must! Gifts had to be exchanged! Indians are very particular about this gifting business, especially the boy's side, which gets most of them. The engagement was fixed for 21 October. Asha and I discussed what she would wear and what I should wear to complement her clothes.

21 October was a mad scramble in the house with the entire Puri family trying to get ready in one bathroom. I was rushing around like a dog on heat.

Suddenly, Bauji said, 'Where do you think you are going?'

'It is my engagement!' I said.

'No, you will not go – you are not required.'

I could not believe what he was saying: I would not be attending my own engagement! This was ridiculous. But he had his own motives. After the engagement there was to be a big *Sangeet* at our residence. Bauji had organised nearly everything, but somebody was required to be present to coordinate things. My brothers were busy distributing wedding cards and making other arrangements. As always, his decision was final. Everybody got ready and left me alone at home. Then, as he got into the car, Bauji told me that I should arrange for about fifty kilos of ice for the soft drinks. How many more tests would I have to

pass before I got my beautiful bride? I had no clue where to get even
one kilo of ice, and fifty kilos was, well! I searched King's Circle, with
no luck. A couple of kilos might have been possible, but fifty? Finally
somebody said there was an ice factory at Dadar (West) beyond the
Gol Temple, and that was where I went, but it was locked. After some
banging at the gate a Gurkha appeared. I told him that I needed ice,
and he said the factory was closed and he was only the *chowkidar*. I
entreated desperately; he relented; he opened the factory, and I saw
dozens of wooden frames, like open coffins filled with water, put
to freeze overnight into hundred kilo blocks. He located a frozen
block and said he could give this to me, but it was a hundred kilos
or nothing. I agreed to take the whole slab, and with the help of the
*chowkidar* and the taxi driver we broke the slab into two and loaded
it into the taxi. I was so relieved I gave the *chowkidar* ₹ 100/- as I
got into the taxi. He said, 'Sir, the ice is only ten paise per kilo and
I do not have change.'

I suggested that he keep the change. He drew himself up to his
full height and said, 'Saab, I will not take advantage of your need.
The amount is ₹ 10/- only so please take your money back and give
me ₹ 10/-.' Humbled by his dignified integrity, I gave him his money
and another ten rupees tip, which he accepted happily.

With the help of the taxi driver I unloaded the two slabs of ice at
the house. They now had to be carried up to the terrace and there was
no help in sight. I took the taxi's jack handle and broke the slabs into
twenty-five kilo pieces, which I carried on my head to the terrace.
On the stairs I met some guests who asked me where the *sangeet*
was? Covering my face, I pointed up the stairs, and heard one of the
ladies tell another,

'Doesn't he look like Sheela's son who is getting married?'

They all laughed and climbed the stairs. The engagement party
returned an hour later along with Asha and some of her family. She
refused to even look at me, and when I finally got in a word, she said
furiously, 'I did not wait for six years to get engaged to your aunt

who wore the ring for me! Now please tell me who I will get married to on the wedding day?'

The *sangeet* carried on till late in the night, and finally, to establish my credentials in Asha's eyes, I announced that I would drop her back home. Both families insisted that she should return with her family, but I was adamant. That did help to re-establish my status in Asha's eyes that I could stand up for my rights.

Many years after our marriage, my father asked Asha why such a beautiful and intelligent girl had fallen in love with a duffer like his son. She blushed and replied that he made her laugh. Bauji said that in that case she should have married Johnny Walker!

# 9 | BAUJI AND RENUKA

In 1966 I brought home my bride. Her name was changed from Asha to Renuka after our wedding because my aunt (Mrs K L Saigal) was also called Asha and lived in the same building. It would have been improper to call my wife by the same name in her presence!

The first part of our honeymoon was at Matheran for a couple of days. We came back home for Diwali and then left for Delhi-Agra-Shimla-Solan for the second phase. Bade Bauji wanted us to stay in our old rented house in Nabha Estate below Shimla Railway Station. It was nice to see the old house and tell Renuka stories of my parents and their life in Shimla, but we preferred to stay at the Grand Hotel on the Mall which cost us ₹ 18/- per day including unlimited breakfast (Defence plus off season concession!).

While in Shimla we learnt that *Shagird*, starring Joy Mukherjee and Saira Banu, was being screened in a local hall. A group of college students sitting ahead of us were vociferous in their condemnation of Madan Puri, especially in a scene where 'Madan, Photographer from Chicago' tries to molest Saira Banu. I could not control myself and shouted at the group to show some restraint. One of them turned round and said, '*Kyon, kya woh tera baap lagta hai?* – Why? Is he your father?'

I quickly realised that this would be a dangerous admission, especially when I had a young wife to protect. I therefore yelled,

'*Maro saale ko*' with the rest. When we returned to Bombay I narrated this story to Bauji and he was pleased as punch. He said that the real reward for actors was when the audience found their performance true to life.

In a similar incident in the late sixties, Renuka accompanied Bauji and Beeji to a film function. Some of the spectators made rude comments about the young woman accompanying my father. Initially Bauji was very upset, but then he realised that the audience had identified Madan Puri with his villainous screen image.

The next halt on our honeymoon was Solan where we stayed with relatives. My grandfather's younger brother Sita Ram chachaji had been the Mohan Meakin Breweries' Chief Brewer. After his early demise his wife and four children lived with Bade Bauji's family, and they all grew up together under his strict and watchful eye. When the Brewery gave her eldest son Purshottam a job, Inder Kaur Puri moved back to Solan to run his bachelor home. We stayed for four days at Solan. In the mornings Renuka and I would walk to the Brewery, drink unlimited Golden Eagle Beer and return home to food made by Bade chachiiji, eaten sitting on the kitchen floor next to the fire. She made the most perfect parothas, topped with blobs of butter, and she recounted stories of her life as she fed us. The memories of shared love and affection – and the weight that we put on in those few days – stayed with us all our lives.

The Army fascinated Bauji. He often told us how he had been invited to join the Officers Training School along with Capt. Nair of Leela Hotels. Had his parents agreed he would have become an officer, served in World War II, and gone on to become a General. The closest he got to his dream was when he joined the Government in the Ministry of Supplies and had some tenuous connections with the war effort. In quite a few movies, such as *Prem Geet*, he acted as a Colonel or a Major and carried a swagger stick. We were highly amused that he wore a 'Kangol' cap and carried a cane when he went for a morning walk. Bauji was very proud of the many trophies adorning our house, especially those that he had received from the Army Chiefs for the fund-raising shows for defence personnel.

This fascination must have rubbed off on us, because Peshi joined the Merchant Navy, while I joined the Army. Bauji visited my brother's ship whenever he got a chance and also visited most of my army stations. He envied us the discipline, the regulated life, the politeness and the aura of authority that surrounded the Defence Services, and was proud of our smart appearance in uniform.

We have a tradition in the Army that when an officer's parents or relativies visit, we arrange a party in the Officers' Mess, or at their residence, or a picnic with all officers and families. My parents visited us at Kota in 1968. On this occasion the Officers' Mess had arranged a party for my parents. All the men were smartly attired and the ladies were dressed to the nines; the lighting was stylishly low-key. The party was going great guns and at the end they asked Bauji to say a few words. He thanked them all and said, 'My daughter-in-law took a lot of pains to get ready and I am sure all you folks have done likewise. In the films when we have a party it is well lit, because everybody wants to see and be seen. Because of your subdued lighting I haven't seen a single face. If we meet another time and I fail to recognise you then please don't put it down to *filmi nakhras*!'

To make up for my father's disappointment, Renuka threw a big party the next day, with bright lights so that her father-in-law could see everybody – and also be seen!

While at Kota I took my parents to meet another Puri family. One of the officers of my Battalion was Major R C Puri whose elder brother was a long time resident of Kota. We met Mr Jagdish Chandra Puri and his family and soon we became inseparable. He had been the farm in-charge of His Highness of Kota and was very popular with the King. When Mr Puri retired the King gifted him the huge house that had been his quarters while in service.

We invited Puri Saab and his family to meet my parents and it was a great meeting of two good men who had hundreds of anecdotes to exchange. He was a Puri from Sialkot while we were Puris from Batala. There were some common relatives and histories.

In the same year our family went to IIT Powai to meet Dalip Laroiya, Sarla aunty's son. At that time Powai was a thick jungle. The road was badly maintained, and it took two hours to get to IIT. It had been a long and emotionally tiring day. As they said goodbye, first Dalip wept, and then Beeji wept, then Renuka wept; then Ramnesh, not to be left out, also wept. Bauji must have wept too because we are the weepy kind of family who display our emotions all the time.

Bauji and Beeji chatted during the drive home. When they reached Sion, Beeji suddenly went silent. As the car turned into the lane, she whispered to Renuka that she had left the almirah keys on Dalip's study table at Powai. She was so petrified that Bauji would be angry that she told Renuka to inform him, and the moment the car stopped, she ran into the house. Renuka gently told Bauji that they would have to drive back to Powai as she had left her purse behind. Bauji said there was no need to go back for a purse that contained only a lipstick and some money. She then told him that the almirah keys were also at Powai and everybody's clothes and money and other items that might be needed the next day were locked up.

Renuka offered to accompany Bauji, but he felt it was a risky journey at night. He went back to Powai with Ramnesh and returned about five hours later. It had been a very long night. Bauji did not say a word to Beeji because he was an understanding and loving man. He might have been short tempered, but his anger was momentary.

# 10 | SAI BABA

Our family's long connection with Sai Baba started in 1956 when Bauji was on an outdoor shoot near Shirdi. He decided to visit the temple. At that time Shirdi was a small dusty village with few visitors, and the only accommodation available was a government guest-house with three sparsely furnished rooms. A beautiful marble statue of the holy man, installed in 1954, exuded peace and tranquility. One could not help but pay obeisance.

Peshi had applied to join T S Dufferin for entry into the Merchant Navy. When Bauji returned from Shirdi the next day, he confidently asked Peshi when he would report for training. We all started laughing, and asked Bauji how he was so sure he had qualified. He said he had received the results from Sai Baba himself! Peshi went on to be a Merchant Navy Captain and served with many companies, national and international. He later joined the Bombay Port Trust as a Harbour Pilot and served for many more years. Finally, he bought his own ships and sailed them for some years.

Sai Baba has repeatedly blessed our family. In the monsoon of 1967, Bauji was shooting back-to-back in Bombay and Delhi. In between he would go to Madras for another shoot. We only got a chance to meet him at the airport, when we handed him an overnight bag containing fresh clothes. He was invariably first off the flight and we felt proud to see him striding down the tarmac, so full of purpose.

When he was back in Bombay after this strenuous period, Bauji had driven to Khandala for an outdoor shoot in his own car and returned home late at night in heavy rain, thoroughly drenched. Wordlessly, he went and changed his clothes and we began dinner. Suddenly he started shivering. He told us that he had just survived a major accident on the highway, when he crashed into a truck abandoned in the middle of the road without warning signs or lights. He walked a couple of miles to the nearest police outpost, where he filed a report and got a policeman placed on duty at the accident site. The next morning Ramnesh and I went to the site and saw that the Standard Herald had gone under the truck right up to its windshield; the steering wheel was bent out of shape, but fortunately the engine block was intact. All that had stood between Bauji and certain death was a small statue of Sai Baba on the dashboard.

We had to deflate the front tires to extricate the car, and arrange for a tow truck to take us to a garage at Portuguese Church. The police frequently stopped us en route, asking how many passengers had died, and where were the dead and injured. It was only my Army Officer's identity card that got us through.

On another occasion, our parents were returning from Shirdi and the driver dozed off at the wheel. The car went over the cliff. Due to Sai Baba's blessings the car stopped on a rocky ledge a few feet below, when it could have fallen a couple of hundred feet. It had to be lifted back onto the road by a crane.

While we were stationed at Mhow in 1974, we decided to go to Bombay via Shirdi. Sonal and Kanchan were in the back seat with our pomeranian, Spotty, and they kept us entertained till we reached Shirdi. We had always come with Bauji and received VIP treatment. This time, my army uniform did not impress the local staff. We had some difficulty getting a room, and our little dog was not welcome. The girls would not let her spend the night alone in the car, so I suggested that I stay with her – but that was also not acceptable. Finally, we all sat in the car with her till late night, and then smuggled her into the room. The food was too spicy for the children, and I could not get milk for them. Mosquitoes kept us awake for most of the night. Next morning, while my wife was getting the girls ready, I decided to do a quick darshan. Having made my obeisance, I said to Sai Baba, 'I have been coming here for many years and have enjoyed each visit. However, this visit has been difficult for my wife and children. In future, I shall never visit this place but shall pay my respects from a distance.' We drove off to Bombay.

Bauji was sitting in his favourite place on the carpet, and was delighted to see us. He said, 'You know, it is amazing and it must surely be Sai Leela. I have no shooting for the next two days, and I have been telling your brothers to take us to Shirdi, but they keep making excuses. You will surely take us, like a good son. I would have gone by myself but the driver is on leave, and my night vision is not so good.'

I could not refuse. Beeji packed a suitcase, and within half an hour we were on our way back to Shirdi. Sai Baba did not even let the sun set on my decision to never visit Shirdi again! I could only bow to his supreme will. We made many visits to Shirdi after that, and we were well received each time.

# 11 | PESHI GETS A BRIDE

Peshi was three years older than me and my mother was getting anxious about him still being unmarried. Messages went out and proposals were received.

A proposal came from Chennai, from a Punjabi family. Peshi's ship was to dock in Chennai after a couple of days and the girl's family was requested to meet him on board the ship. Peshi was not particularly keen on marriage but agreed to meet the family. The girl's father came to the ship and insisted that Peshi should have a meal with them at a prominent hotel. Peshi fetched up with a sailor friend. Some serious naval style drinking followed and finally Peshi and his friend escorted the girl's father to his room and tucked him into bed. A couple of days later the girl's father informed my parents that he had enjoyed meeting Peshi and was keen on moving forward but was dismayed to find that he enjoyed his drinks a little too much. Peshi had already informed Beeji about the meeting. Like a tigress Beeji rushed to the defence of her son. She said that our family would not like to carry this proposal further, and in any case the girl's father was hardly a shining example of a teetotaller.

Some weeks later Bauji went to Delhi for a film premiere. He was also to meet the family of a young lady whose father was well spoken of. The film was a success and everybody was in a mood to celebrate. There were the usual businessmen, socialites, hangers on and young women out for a good time. The young hero with the irresistible smile was the centre of attraction. One particularly vivacious young woman caught his attention and after some time they left the party together.

The next morning Bauji picked up his sister Kanta Mehra to take her to meet the family. She had brought a photograph of the girl and when Bauji saw it he was dismayed. She was the vivacious young lady who had ridden into the sunset with the young hero the night before! Bauji and Kanta aunty decided not to pursue the proposal. When Bauji returned home he told my horrified mother about Peshi's lucky escape.

The search for a bride for Peshi finally led to the home of late Lt Col B R Mehta. Colonel Mehta had passed away at an early age of a cardiac arrest. Veena was the youngest of four siblings; two of her brothers were in the Army and the third was in the Air Force. The wedding was held with great pomp and show in Delhi, followed by a grand reception.

Bauji's first grandchild, Kanchan, was born on 25 January 1969. It was a great day for our family. On the same day we received two other gifts: a new Ambassador car from B R Chopra Films, and a spitz puppy named Spotty from Shakti Samantha Saab. A year later Spotty produced a litter of six puppies. Bauji got emotional, saying that all the puppies must stay at home. Finally, adamant that nothing would be charged for the pups, he agreed to give them away, but insisted on interviewing all the prospective owners.

One day Bauji suggested to me that now that there were three members in my family, I should sell my motorcycle and buy a car. He offered to pay for the car. I thanked him but declined. Most of my army colleagues could barely afford scooters and motorcycles and I did not want to buy a car until I could pay for it. Bauji was happy and proud (and perhaps relieved) at my refusal. He felt that a man should live within his means.

# THE INDO-PAK WAR 1971

During the 1971 Indo-Pak War I was posted on the Western Front. Renuka and Kanchan were in Bombay with my parents. The war was brief but intense, especially in the Chhamb sector. My battalion was awarded some medals for bravery. During the war Bauji had tried to find out my location, but was stumped because my regiment had three Puris apart from me: M S Puri, R C Puri and S K S Puri. His enquiry was always about 'Puri's' location! As a result all location reports gave differing positions. Bauji discussed the matter with his good friend Sunil Dutt, who was planning to take his Ajanta Arts troupe to the border areas after the fighting was over. The ceasefire was declared on 17 December 1971. Sunil Dutt zeroed in on Chhamb because that was my last sighted location. The troupe was a great morale booster for the troops, and for me it was a glimpse of home in the war zone. My family was both relieved and overjoyed when I came home on 31 December 1971, in time for Kanchan's third birthday.

My father had a very amused look on his face at the airport. He told me that for the past month my mother had hardly eaten, my elder brother was fasting every day and was glued to the radio for news from the war zone, and my wife was silent and depressed. Yet, said my father, here I was, rosy-cheeked and looking disgracefully healthy, a reprise of our return from Pathankot in the Calcutta days!

I was perhaps one of the first soldiers to return from the battlefield, and there were press interviews and parties galore. But I had been changed by my experience. I had seen young friends, officers and soldiers die. I had seen the enemy die. Then they were neither friend nor foe, nor Hindu nor Muslim, just bodies. Once you have seen death at close quarters it loses its terror, and becomes another journey.

In 1973, Bauji had not been keeping well and the doctor advised a change of weather and a strict diet. My parents flew to Delhi and I came from my Duty Station in Ambala. We drove up to Nainital for a week's stay, but without Renuka. She had gone to Bombay with Kanchan to sit out the last few weeks of her second pregnancy. On the first evening, we took a walk and also went for a movie. During the interval, I went to fetch some snacks. On my return I found Bauji surrounded by fans. They started discussing who I was, and one of the more knowledgeable ones said (quite loudly), '*Arre yaar*, all film stars move around with their *chamchas*!'

That evening, Bauji called the waiter and told him to bring one plate of everything on the menu. Beeji protested, but Bauji said, 'I have had enough of the doctor's advice. If I have to die, then let it be after a hearty meal!'

The next day, he declared that he was bored and wanted to go back to Bombay, which was not acceptable to my mother and me. That evening we learnt that Dharmendra Saab was on a shoot in Nainital. We promptly fetched up at Dharmendra's hotel. He was in the lobby, gossiping with his friends and being ogled by the women.

Dharmendrea was delighted to see Bauji and said, 'Chachaji, I need your advice; there is a newly married couple at the bar and the woman is eyeing me continuously. Will it be the husband or me tonight?'

Bauji admonished him, saying, 'My son is also here, so be careful what you say.'

Dharmendra turned round and said to me, 'Betaji, you please go and sit somewhere else as we are having an adult conversation.'

Bauji said that I was a Major in the army. Promptly Dharmendra responded: 'In that case Major Saab, please join us, have a drink and give us your considered opinion on my query.'

I had mentioned to Bauji that it would be nice if we knew somebody at the Nainital Club. We could then be introduced as guests and buy ourselves some drinks. A moment later a gentleman introduced himself as an admirer of Bauji and invited us for a drink. He was Mr Mandelia of Century Rayon. We had a pleasant evening and my mother also enjoyed meeting his wonderful family. The remaining three days of our stay found us regularly at the club at 6 pm. The friendship with the Mandelias continued when we returned to Bombay.

# 12 | KANCHAN AND SONAL

Our second daughter Sonal was delivered on 2 August 1973 by emergency caesarean. The rains were very heavy during the first week of August, and it was nearly impossible to reach the maternity home, a mile away in Hindu Colony, Dadar. In spite of the tension Bauji kept his cool, and his place on the carpet was the rallying point for the family.

In 1974, I was posted at Mhow (MP) as a teacher at the Army War College. We had a rambling old house, which has since been converted to a Central School. Our old sitting room is now the school assembly hall.

Due to Bauji's shooting commitments my parents were unable to attend Sonal's first birthday party, and arrived a few days later. Bauji, who had always claimed to be an outdoorsman because of his early years in Shimla, expressed his happiness to be in the (near) outdoors. I had planned no social events as he had mentioned that he wanted a quiet holiday. As darkness fell on the first evening we sat around having a drink on the front lawn. Suddenly, we heard the baying of wolves. Bauji quietly asked if there were a lot of stray dogs in the vicinity. Kanchan, aged six, said, 'Daadu, those are wolves.'

Nothing more was said, but next morning Bauji wanted to catch the first flight to Bombay. He had spent his adult life in Calcutta and Bombay and now suddenly he was visiting a cantonment area where jackals and sometimes even leopards and panthers were seen! However, we did arrange a series of parties where he could be a roaring lion himself, eyeing the innocent lambs in sarees and salwar kameez.

My parents and Ramnesh visited us in 1976 at the Defence Services Staff College, Wellington. We received them at Coimbatore Airport. We planned to drive along the Kerala coast down to Kanya Kumari, back along the eastern coast to Coimbatore, and then up to Wellington, a beautiful hill station twenty-five kilometers short of Ooty. Our Fiat car was very heavily loaded with five adults, two children, one dog and mountains of baggage. The Fiat was a brave-heart, but the retreaded tyres were her Achilles heel and gave way after the first hundred kilometers. Bauji paid for four new tyres. He then asked me if the battery required replacement, and what about the engine overhauling? Then surely I would need to get the car painted and the seats refurbished after the trip…

It was a great trip except for the temple visits. Some temples insisted that the men entered bare-chested. My father wore a heavy gold chain and a rudraksh mala, but he did not want to expose his body. At every temple we had an argument. After seven days of cramped traveling, we returned to Conoor. In the evening, Kanchan and Sonal took their Daadu to Sim's Park for a walk, and he told them about the horrible walks-cum-study sessions with his father in Simla.

During the vacations it was parties galore – up to six cocktail parties in an evening! This was not as expensive as it could have been because the army wives did most of the preparations at home, everybody bought liquor from the canteen, and nobody overindulged. Then the host would spend the next month attending parties at his friends' homes, so expenses got balanced out. The invitees were a mix of students and instructors and their wives.

Everybody, no matter how sophisticated, wants to meet a film actor. At nearly every party, Bauji was told that Staff College was a very difficult course and everybody had to study very hard. He expressed his doubts, citing the number of parties he had so far attended! Renuka threw a gala party at our residence with about a hundred and fifty invitees. Bauji complimented her, saying, 'You have been in our family for ten years and now I see you in your element. You army wives mix with everybody and yet maintain your dignity. My son is very lucky and so are we.'

James Bond's escapades and attempts to break through the Iron Curtain are legendary, but what is less well known is that our Madan 'Bond' achieved this feat during his visit to Tashkent during the shooting of F C Mehra's *Ali Baba aur Chalis Chor*. After completing his shooting, Madan 'Bond' took a flight to Moscow, a city he had always wanted to see. Once he had checked into the hotel, he went sightseeing the whole day. In the evening he went to the hotel bar for a beer. An attractive young Russian lady came and sat next to him. 'You are Madan Puri, a film actor from Bombay,' she said in perfect English. Bemused, Bauji nodded. 'I have been following you the whole day,' she said, and listed the places he had visited. Bauji must have looked as puzzled as he probably felt, for she added, 'It is our normal practice to watch our guests and ensure their safety. Tomorrow there will be somebody else on duty, and I shall ask him to introduce himself and take you around.' She refused a drink, and left.

That was as far as the 'Bond' activities went. The following day he went sightseeing again, with an amiable watchdog to show him around, and in the evening he took the Aeroflot flight back to India. While the plane was still over Russian airspace it was intercepted by a couple of Russian fighter aircraft and directed to land at the nearest airport. The police entered the plane and demanded to know who Madan Puri was. At this point the script changed and Bond Saab went a little weak at the knees. Apparently he had somehow left Moscow without getting his exit visa stamped! This had created a security scare, which led to the interception. The police wanted Bauji to return to Moscow with them. After a lot of explanations and pleading and the invocation of 'Hindi-Russi Bhai-Bhai', Jawaharlal

Nehru and Nargis-Raj Kapoor, the police relented, Bauji's visa was stamped and the aircraft proceeded to India, with Bauji brooding over his narrow escape.

Sonal had asked Bauji to bring her a walkie-talkie doll. He could only find Russian-speaking dolls, so he bought her a teddy bear instead. It was Sonal's constant companion until she left for USA in 1995 for higher studies.

Sonal has fond memories of her affectionate grandfather: 'Every year we came to Bombay for our vacations, and Bauji would take time out for the children. He would take us for drives and buy us ice cream. Sometimes we went to Juhu beach, which was not very crowded even on Sundays. We enjoyed our swim and then went to our flat near the beach, where we showered and ate lunch. One Sunday, we were surprised when we entered the flat to find a famous young film star very much at home. She was even more surprised than us. Bauji had given the key to Ramnesh chachu, who had given a duplicate to the actress. After some polite conversation the young lady got up to leave. Bauji was careful to take the key from her before she left.

'In the evenings we used to play in the Lane; Papa would give Kanchan and me one rupee each to buy *bhel* or *paani-puri*. If Bauji was at home he gave us five rupees each and then we would totally pig out. Bauji was particular about the clothes we wore; he did not approve of skirts and frocks and preferred us to wear *salwar-kameez* or track pants.

'Whenever our grandparents came to visit us they would bring lots of gifts. Our neighbours and friends would come to meet him, and Kanchan and I would run up and down looking after the guests, feeling very important.'

# 13 | THE CENTRE OF OUR UNIVERSE

Bauji had made the threshold of his house like a Lakshman Rekha: his professional socialising took place outside the house, and we never saw filmwallahs at home. He always said, 'I love the film industry and it is my bread and butter but I would like to shield my family from it, at least till my sons are older.'

Later, Bauji was equally protective of his grandchildren. They never visited the film studios, nor were they introduced to anyone from the film world. Whenever 'filmi' guests arrived, his granddaughters were sent to their rooms.

For Bauji his family came first. There was nothing that he would not do to keep us happy; the family was not just his wife and children but the entire *Khandaan* – he had learned from his father that this was his duty, and he loved doing it. Whenever he had an evening off he would call the family over for dinner. Even when Bauji was departing for his eternal journey, the whole family was at his bedside praying with him.

My father came from a family with great *parampara*. He always spoke with great pride of his cousin sister, Saraswati Uppal, who lived with her husband and children in a huge bungalow at No 1, Keeling Road, Delhi. My father's younger sister Chandrakanta was to be married to Mr Rajesh Chandra Mehra and it was decided that all the celebrations would be held at Saraswati aunty's house. Mr Uppal was very unwell and confined to bed. On the day of the marriage we assembled in the lawns to receive the *baraat*. *Shehnais* were playing and children were running around excitedly like small puppies. The servant attending Mr Uppal came and spoke softly to Saraswati aunty. She went to their bedroom and found that her husband had just breathed his last. She could hear the revelry at the corner of the lane. She swore the servant to secrecy, locked her bedroom, put the AC on full blast and went outside to receive the *baraat*. The whole night passed in joy and laughter and Saraswati aunty was part of the revelry. The grand function finished in the early hours of the morning with the departure of the *doli*. When the last guest had been seen off with all honors, Saraswati aunty broke down and informed her children and my grandfather about the tragedy that had struck the family. She told my grandfather, 'Today one of your daughters has become a *suhagan* and the other has become an *abhagan*. Please do your duty and take your other son-in-law to the cremation grounds.'

My father told this story to us and to his daughters-in-law many times, impressing upon us the importance of family values, and the greatness of Saraswati aunty.

Bauji was the centre of our universe, as I came to realise after I became a parent. Like most mothers, Beeji looked after us 24/7, but Bauji was still the centre, and Beeji kept him fully informed about our activities. He acted directly only in extreme circumstances for which I, more than my other two brothers, gave him ample opportunity. Bauji was physically very strong. Even in his late sixties, he could catch my elder brother by one wrist and me with the other hand and challenge us to break free. No matter how hard we tried, we could never succeed. This display of strength made us feel proud and very secure.

The family always ate dinner together, no matter how late, for this was often the only time we got together in the whole day. After dinner we played cards, sitting on the carpet while the children sprawled on the sofas and read books or comics or just watched us. Bauji always won. He never let his sons play as they refused to pay up their losses. It was great fun being together. The whole family would stay awake till about 0200. He would then tell his daughters-in-law, 'OK, I am tired, so good night. Come back tomorrow evening when your husbands have earned some more money.' The next morning he would distribute the winnings of the previous night between his two daughters-in-law.

Ludo was another matter. Beeji was the family champion. Bauji could never get a 6 to start his moves, while Beeji romped home. In Snakes and Ladders too, the snake sitting around the 60's always bit Bauji and he would return to 2. After Bauji tore up a couple of expensive boards we bought a half dozen of the two-anna types to cater for 'Dad's Bad Days'.

Bauji was generous with his family, without permitting any extravagance. He gave all his earnings to Beeji and let her handle the details. Periodically, to assert his authority, he would tell Beeji sternly, 'OK, I gave you five thousand last week, now give me the account.' She would say, 'I have spent four rupees for onions, two rupees for tomatoes...' and the list went on and on without any item being over ten rupees. After a few minutes she would have enumerated about two hundred rupees expenditure but it sounded like so much more. Bauji had been tricked once again! He would bring her some money the next day.

Beeji was not easy to fool; after all she was the daughter of a successful businessman. She knew that the film world does not guarantee a steady income so every month she quietly put away some money. I discovered this in a very comical way. I had to go to Pune from Chandigarh on a short training course. En route I stopped in Bombay and asked my mother for some bedding. She gave me a mattress, a blanket, a couple of sheets and a pillow. On reaching Pune, I placed my luggage in my room in the Officers Mess. After dinner I made my bed and felt a lump in the pillow. It was a bundle of currency notes! After a disturbed night I called home. When I mentioned the pillow, Beeji said we would discuss when we met, and said a hurried 'Bye'. The following weekend I went to Bombay and gave her the money. She explained how she saved for a rainy day – and it can rain very heavily in the film industry. I cannot recollect a single occasion when Bauji took a financial decision without consulting Beeji.

Bauji was a contented man. He had no greed, no jealousy and he never craved for anything. He always said, 'Until the money is not in my pocket it is not mine.' He then added ruefully, 'But once it is in my pocket, your mother takes it away!'

After Bauji's demise, many people from financially poor backgrounds came to convey their condolences and they told us how Bauji had quietly helped them out during some financial crisis.

Bauji was politically aware and socially conscious, and for a short time was a member of the local Congress District Committee. In the early fifties he had spearheaded a move to have a Locality Security Organisation. He and Beeji voted regularly and took part in all local social activities. Bauji always voted Congress, while Beeji voted for the Jan Sangh.

Bauji had a temper but he also knew how to keep it under control. One day, I called a passing cobbler and gave him a suitcase for repairs. The job was not done according to my instructions. I berated the man harshly and sent him off after paying him the agreed amount. After the man left my father told me in a soft but firm voice that he was concerned because I had been very harsh to the man. It is a fact that I have always been short tempered and this has often created complications in my personal and professional life. Perhaps, if I had heeded my father's advice, I may have been well served in life.

When my daughters were growing up, Bauji worried about whether I could manage with such a meagre salary. He suggested a monthly educational allowance for the girls. He was very happy when I refused the offer. We had put the girls in the *Kendriya Vidyalayas* where the standard of education was good, regular transfers were not a hassle and the fees were minimal. Bauji then suggested that I opened an account with the nearby bank, and left the cheque-book and passbook with him. He would put money in whenever he had some to spare. When I returned he studied the passbook and was shocked to find an opening entry of ₹ 10/-. I explained that I had planned to open the account with ₹ 5/-, but the bank manager said ₹ 10/- was the minimum amount required to be eligible for a cheque-book! Like a certain British queen, Bauji was not amused.

In 1981 Sanjay Khan's *Abdullah* was being shot at Jodhpur and Bauji had a small part in the movie. I was on leave, so he took me along. We flew to Delhi to catch a night train to Jodhpur. At Delhi we learnt that all trains were cancelled due to a railway strike. Madan Puri never gave up easily. We took a taxi to Jodhpur so that the shooting schedule would not be upset. It meant traveling the whole night through the desert with little help available in case of a breakdown. However Bauji was confident of his own abilities to take on any risk; besides, he had his soldier son for company and protection. We started off. The protection party promptly went to sleep while he maintained the same level of high alertness during the entire journey.

We arrived at the Palace Hotel in the wee hours of the morning. The shoot was scheduled to start at sunrise, and we tried to get a little sleep. An hour later Bauji heard noises and put on the light. I had noted the beautiful brass poker set in the fireplace; now I was trying to fit it into my suitcase. Astounded, he asked me what I was doing.

'Collecting antiques,' I said simply.

Bauji never indulged in abuse and his favourite (and only) words of anger were *ullu ka patha* and *kutte ka bacha*. I now received many such words of endearment both for my actions and for having disturbed his sleep. By then it was time to get ready and move to the site, about fifteen kilometres from Jodhpur. Once he had settled me down he went off for the shoot as if he had rested the whole night. An hour later he came to check on my comfort and found me sitting with an army friend and a couple of young ladies. The officer was posted at

Jodhpur and had convinced the ladies that he knew Madan Puri's son very well. Imagine his surprise when he actually saw me there! I was happy to assist, as the girls were quite pretty. Bauji was amazed at the camaraderie of the Defence Services.

In 1981, we vacationed in Shimla, and Bauji pointed out to my daughters the places on the Mall where he had learnt Maths and Urdu grammar from his father. He had a great time meeting old friends and reliving old memories. During this visit, we stayed overnight at the Army Inspection Bungalow. As we left next morning I gave the *chowkidar* a hundred-rupee note, with a flourish. Bauji was quiet till we had driven some distance. Then he said he was surprised that I had given *baksheesh* of a hundred rupees. When I told him that the hundred covered the cost of two deluxe rooms, plus dinner, bed tea, and breakfast for six, he suggested that we should go back to the bungalow as it was cheaper than living at home in Bombay!

Bauji was proud of his home and the fact that his wife and children had a secure life. He made it a point of always being available for us. He was satisfied with life and grateful to God for whatever he had received. He touched us all in a very positive manner. During his lifetime he had moved the entire family up through many financial and social levels and had given us all an identity: I am the brother/son/nephew of Madan Puri. His virtues and good habits are very much a part of our own. He was a man of true principles, noble values, ethics and morals. He respected people for what they were and never belittled or demeaned anybody.

Bauji was good looking, polite and cultured; we could not compare with him in looks, vitality or charisma. He was restrained and dignified in all his actions. The streak of austerity came from his father. It is to his credit that he was able to balance his glamorous professional life with that of a middle class family.

# 14 | BAUJI AND RAMNESH

Bauji had managed to shield his two older sons from the film world, and had entrepreneurial plans for Ramnesh. Bauji was keen that his youngest son should obtain a degree in electronic engineering and set up a TV manufacturing unit. Ramnesh wanted to join the IAF and become a pilot, which was not acceptable to the family.

One day Ramnesh drove Bauji to the sets of Shakti Saab's *Aradhana* at Natraj Studio, where he met Shakti Samanta, Rajesh Khanna, Sharmila Tagore, and also Babu Arora, an old friend who was assisting Shakti Saab. Ramnesh was mesmerized by his first visit to a studio and wanted to be a part of it all. When Bauji came on the set for his scene he was surprised to see Ramnesh still there. Shakti Saab suggested to Bauji that Ramnesh should be allowed to stay for the day, so he stayed on and helped Babu write the continuity sheet. Next day Ramnesh told Beeji that he did not want to study any more, but wanted to become a film director. One never spoke to Bauji directly on such matters; it was always through Beeji, so that she could charm Bauji into agreeing!

A couple of days later Bauji requested Shakti Saheb to take Ramnesh under his wing. Once it was decided that he would work in the Industry, Bauji laid down some rules:

- *Ramnesh would not use his father's name to get out of any situation, or to gain any benefit.*

- *Whatever transpired in the work place would stay there.*
- *One can inherit wealth and property but name and fame you have to earn for yourself.*
- *So go and work hard.*
- *You will never abandon an assignment that you have accepted unless you are asked to leave, nor should you do anything that will cause the company to throw you out.*
- *Never cry over spilt milk; start thinking of a solution or an alternative.*
- *Money makes a man rich but not necessarily wise.*
- *Never cancel a confirmed date with one company in order to oblige some other producer.*
- *Never use abusive language.*

Ramnesh worked for Shakti Films during their golden years. He was an Assistant Director for *Aradhana* (1968), *Jaane Anjaane* (1968), *Kati Patang* (1971), *Charitraheen*(1971), *Amar Prem* (1972), *Anuraag* (1974), *Ajnabee* (1975).

He later struck out independently and made *Raftaar* (1975), *Naani Bai Ko Mairo*, *Zulm Ki Pukar* (1979), *Aakhri Kasam* (1979), *Tejaa* (1986) and *Madadagar* (1987).

Ramnesh launched his first independent venture *Raftaar* (1975) with Vinod Mehra, Moushami Chatterji, Madan Puri and others.

Bauji played the role of a musician who had lost his daughter in a boat accident, but continued to celebrate her birthday every year.

The heroine (played by Moushami Chatterji) takes the place of the dead daughter in the birthday party. The song that Bauji was to sing was the centrepiece of a very emotional scene: '*Sansar hai ek nadiya, dukh sukh do kinare hain. Na jaane kahan jaye, hum baehti dhaara hain.*'

Ramnesh explained the situation to Bauji, and his part in the song. Bauji was in a panic, 'You want me to act, sing, and play this violin moving my fingers and the bow... All in one go. You are crazy.'

However, Ramnesh sent out his staff to look for a professional violinist, who returned with one Mr Collins Gomez whom they had found playing for a wedding party. Gomez had agreed to come on hearing that they were shooting a birthday scene.

Gomez was welcomed, but took a stand: First give me a drink and then we will talk. Ramnesh told Gomez that he would get whatever he wished but first he had to do he what he had come for, to which he reluctantly agreed.

Gomez showed Bauji how to hold the violin and the bow, and when Bauji did it badly, he became angry, saying, 'Man, this is a musical instrument and not a bazooka, and that is a bow and not a hockey stick!'

Gomez was tense and asked for 'Petrol' to keep him going. The production boys kept fulfilling his demands. Bauji was willing to humour him till the work was done. Soon a somewhat inebriated Gomez was not only teaching Bauji the violin but also showing him how he could dance to the tune.

On the completion of the song the production staff gave Gomez a case of rum and sent him off very happy. A few days later Gomez landed up at our home and suggested that the violin lessons should continue. Madan Puri now played his most villainous role, and we never saw Gomez again.

In 1983, Ramnesh married Gayatri, daughter of Colonel and Mrs P B Singh. The wedding was held in Jaipur. I had just been posted to Kota, and Jaipur was about five hours' drive away. It was a wonderful opportunity to have the entire family visit us. Chaman tayaji and family, Sarla aunty and family, Amrish chachaji and family, Harish chachaji and family, Peshi, Veena and Vicky, my maternal uncles from Pathankot, and some more relatives all came to stay.

The Army came to the rescue and helped me get some guest rooms in Kota. I arranged for some cooks and waiters and we were set. Local family friends like the J C Puri family and Lt Col D N Sharma and family and the officers of the Kota Garrison joined in the festivities.

The moment my parents arrived and entered their room, Bauji lay down on the bed and told Renuka, 'We are guests at your brother-in-law's wedding and it is entirely your show. Please tell your husband that we expect him to meet all expenses!'

Renuka rose to the challenge magnificently. For the Jaipur trip she prepared and packed lunches and dinners for forty *baraatis*. Kanchan and Sonal helped to serve everyone, and told all the neighbours that we had Chaman Puri, Madan Puri and Amrish Puri staying with us. Since our house was right in the centre of the crowded Collectorate area, we caused some horrendous traffic jams.

We hired a private bus for the drive to Jaipur, and thanks to Renuka's cooking we stopped for lunch and tea wherever we wanted. Gayatri's family received us at Jaipur in the traditional Rajasthani style of *Mehmaan Nawaz* with bugles and horses. I was unable to concentrate much on the festivities because Bauji had so far made no move to reimburse any of our expenses. I had padded up the bills so that I could make some extra money in the process. This misery continued till we returned to Kota and he decided to clear my bills. We all took the train to Bombay to attend the Reception.

The reception was held at Hotel Sea Lord at Juhu. Bauji had invited the entire film world, and they all came. It was a joyous moment in his life. At the end of the day he felt satisfied that his colleagues had honoured him with their attendance. None of us could have guessed it, but that was the last major event that he would host.

# 15 | CHAMAN, MADAN, AMRISH

Ours was a small but fortunate house, always overflowing with guests and relatives. From 1947 until about 1955, Chaman tayaji and his family stayed with us. Before Partition, Chaman tayaji had gone to Lahore to try his luck in films, without much success, and then decided to move to Bombay to try his luck again. I once asked him about Lahore and whether he had visited the famous Heera Mandi. He smiled and said that he had certainly feasted his eyes.

Heera Mandi in Lahore, now a red-light area, was once the center of the city's *tawaif* culture. Courtesans used to be hired by wealthy families to teach their children social behavior and etiquette. However, over time, the aesthetic pursuit was diluted. The British developed the brothel houses. During the day the place is much like other Pakistani bazaars and is known for its good food, wide range of traditional Mughal footwear and shops for musical instruments.

Chaman tayaji's family in Bombay comprised Satyavati aunty, two daughters, Aruna and Ritoo, and his son Anoop. Another son Sunil was born later. His two older sons Pradip and Vinod were living in Delhi with our grandparents. One of our two bedrooms went to tayaji's family; the other bedroom was ours. The sitting room carpet was reserved for other guests. In those days nobody made a fuss about things like separate bedrooms; everybody sat around and gossiped and recounted family tales, had their meals and went to sleep wherever space was available.

In 1954, Pradip and Vinod also came to live in Bombay. It was difficult for eight people to stay in one room. A flat was purchased at Malad and tayaji moved there with his family. Once a month, my mother would take Peshi and me to Malad to visit our cousins.

The move to Malad proved very unfortunate for tayaji. Sunil died of diptheria when he was about eight years old. A year later Pradip died in a scooter accident, aged twenty-one. This broke tayaji's spirit. He suddenly aged and lost his zest for life. His wife was perpetually sick and depressed after these emotional blows. They however maintained a calm and graceful façade in spite of their grief, and tayaji lavished his love on the children of the entire family.

Our paternal grandmother passed away in 1958 in Delhi after a long and debilitating illness. Bauji received the message at the studio where, ironically, he was shooting a scene where he and his cronies were sitting and jeering at the hero, whose mother had died, and the police had brought him to the funeral in handcuffs. Chaman tayaji was shooting at the same studio. Bauji did not tell him immediately, because he was afraid that tayaji would break down and his shooting would have to be cancelled. Instead, he informed the producer, telling him that both of them would be leaving for Delhi that night and would not return for a few days. He advised the producer that he should complete the maximum work with tayaji before the news broke. It was only after the pack-up that he told tayaji, and then they both broke down and cried. Bauji was only three years younger than tayaji. They had grown up and lived in Bombay for many years, and also worked and socialized together. Bauji was always polite and respectful towards his elder brother, and for that matter I never saw Amrish chachaji ever behave otherwise than a respectful younger brother towards tayaji and Bauji.

Tayaji had a wonderful tale about friendship. When in 1945 he resigned from the American Company where he was working to seek his future in films, they presented him with a Parker Dufold pen. One day a friend took the pen from tayaji and playfully said that he would keep it. Some days passed, and in the confusion of packing and leaving for Pakistan, the pen remained with the friend. Many decades passed, and the pen and the friend became a distant memory tinged with regret. In the early nineties, tayaji's friend visited India and managed to locate my uncle. When they met he said, 'Chaman, one of my main reasons to visit India was to return your *amanat*. For nearly forty years I have kept this pen carefully in the hope that one day I will return it to you. Our nations have divided but friendships should never suffer.' Tayaji presented me his precious pen when I completed my Ph.D. in 1995. He had never used it, nor had his friend in Pakistan. It remains safely with me, still unused, to be passed on as a family heirloom.

Chaman tayaji passed away in 2003.

Chaman tayaji's film bibliography is hopelessly incomplete. A limited list is appended:

*Deepak* (2000), Aulad (1987), *Pyaar Jhukta Nahin* (1985), *Ek Chitti Pyar Bhari* (1985), *Masoom* (1983), *Bombay 405 miles* (1980), *Kaajal* (1980), *Do Musafir* (1978), *Nawab Sahib* (1978), *Vaangar* – Punjabi (1977), *Saal Solvan Chadiya* – Punjabi (1977), *Ram Bharose* (1977), *Fakira* (1976), *Aap Beati* (1976), *Chori Mera Kaam* (1975), *Chor Machaye Shor* (1974), *Ghulam Begum Badshah* (1973), *Teen Chor* (1973), *Jungle Mein Mangal* (1973), *Victoria No 203* (1972), *Paraya Dhan* (1971), *The Train* (1971), *Jwala* (1971), *Naadan* (1971), *Sansar* (1971), *Geet* (1970), *Insaan aur Shaitan* (1970), *Aan Milo Sajna* (1970), *Chanchal ka Sapna* (1970), *Chor ke Ghar Chor* (1970), *Mastana* (1970), *Taalash* (1969), *Waaris* (1969), *Jhuk Gaya Aasman* (1968), *Ayega Aanewala* ((1967), *Naujawan* (1966), *Pyar Kiye Jaa* (1966), *Shaheed* (1965), *Leader* (1964), *Phool Bane Angarey* (1963), *Mamta* (1963), *Pardesi Dhola* – Punjabi (1962), *Raaz ki Baat* (1962), *Ek Musafir Ek Hasina* (1962), *Hum Matwale Naujawan* (1961), *Tanhai* (1961), *Rahgir* (1961), *Patang* (1960), *Ustad Pedro* (1960), *Hum Bhi Insaan Hain* (1959), *Commander* (1959), *Forty Days* (1959), *Howrah Bridge* (1958), *Sakshi Gopal* (1957), *Aasha*

(1957), *Paying Guest* (1957), *Jalti Nishani* (1957), *Jhanak Jhanak Paayal Baaje* (1956), *Heer* (1956), *Leader* (1954), *Shart* (1954), *Sangam* (1954), *Tulsidas* (1954), *Gguhar* (1953), *Aanso* (1953), *Goonj* (1952), *Nadaan* (1951), Bahar (1951), *Afsana* (1951), *Raat Ki Rani* (1949), *Twenty Six January, Khyber, Mere Saajan, Bahen, Nirmohi, Pyar ka Pehla Sawan.*

Amrish Puri came to Bombay in the early fifties after his graduation and stayed with us. Bauji tried his very best to get Amrish chachaji into the movies but with no success. The producers turned him down because he did not have 'poster boy' looks. Amrish chachaji then joined government service, and after hours worked in theatre where he earned great renown. It was good to watch him working with such determination to make a film career. Every morning he worked out at the gym. After office hours he went for theatre rehearsals and got home late at night. In 1959, he married Ms Urmila Diwaker, who is one of the finest women to walk this earth. She was his office colleague in the Employee State Insurance Corporation. Around 1965, he moved from Masani Road to his own house in Santa Cruz along with his wife and two children, Rajeev and Namrata.

Chachaji's luck changed when Shyam Benegal and Govind Nihalani started making art films like *Ankur* and *Nishant*. His moment arrived with the release of *Mr India* and thereafter *Mogambo Khush Hua.*

Bauji was shooting at Shree Sound Studios, Dadar, when Dev Saab, Pran Saab, Chaman tayaji and Amrish chachaji came to wish him on his birthday. An impromptu party was organized and a car was sent to fetch my mother.

Amrish chachaji, speaking about Madan Puri after his death said, 'As an actor, I think, he was like a musician who knew all the ragas. He could play anything. His sense of comedy was fantastic. He was a very emotional man and his affection for all of us in the family was abounding. His love also flowed over to his larger family – the film industry. He introduced me to some people in the film industry but he used to tell me that the truth was that you could not push somebody through influence. He said, "In Life, the more you crave for something, the more you are denied.""

(Movie / February 1985).

Amrish chachaji has spelt out his life and views in his book *The Act of Life,* co-authored with Jyoti Sabharwal and published by Stellar Publishers Pvt. Ltd, 2006.

Amrish chachaji passed away on 12 January 2005.

# 16 | ALOO-PYAAZ

Bauji once told Randhir Kapoor, 'Movies run on the stars and the producers. The rest of the cast is only required to fill in the blanks. We are like the *Aloo-Pyaaz* that can be put into any dish.'

The top guns of the film world are the stars; men and women of exceptional beauty or great talent or great connections. Bunny Reuben in his book *Follywood Flashback* referred to them as the Beautiful People. They represent the Ideal. Despite his mournful demeanour, Humphrey Bogart became a leading man, but he repudiated the title of 'Star'. Bogart saw a distinct divide between movie stars and actors. To him, stars burned bright and beautiful, but were little more than pretty balls of gas – and he wasn't speaking astronomically!

Bauji used to give effortless performances. His versatility lay in the fact that in each film he tried to portray a different character with different mannerisms. He consistently worked on his craft. I recollect seeing him rehearsing his dialogues in front of the mirror while sitting on the carpet and shaving. He did not enjoy being typecast as a 'villain', but then he had no choice in the matter. Amrish Puri says in his autobiography that when he has to emote a particular scene, 'I can only describe him in superlative terms, because even now, I try and imagine as to how Madan Bhai Saab would have done it and then I get charged... he was a marvelously instinctive actor.' The Jailer of Manoj Kumar's *Shaheed* was very different from the John

Wong of Shakti Samantha's *Howrah Bridge*. Who can imagine that the Madan Babu of Shakti Saheb's *Amar Prem* was the same actor as the Dadajee of *Dulhan Wohi Jo Piya Man Bhaye*? This is perhaps the reason why stage mimics are never able to copy him.

Shivaji Ganesan said, 'The markings of a good actor stand out when he is able to slip in and out of his character, without actually being touched by it, no matter, what the circumstances. That is why I implore actors not to get emotionally attached to their roles. There is no such thing as a small or big part in the acting profession. Even if an actor appears in one scene, his performance should be outstanding and remembered for all time. In films, every new character or director or new co-star makes it a new experience and that is what every new film is for me. If one has a know-it-all attitude without deeming it a challenge, one is sure to slip and fall. On the other hand if we take every new project as a new experience and work hard with self-confidence, we shall surely climb the ladder of success' (as recorded by Dr T S Narayanswami in the biography of Shivaji Ganeshan).

Comparing the making of a film to the building of a table, Director Frank Capra (1897–1991) once said: 'On the top of my table, which is bright and shiny, I have these lovely dolls that are my leading actors and actresses. But it is not a table until I put legs under it, and those are my character people. That's what holds my picture up. When the character actor shows his brilliance partly because he got plenty of freedom to apply his creativity and partly because the role was strongly defined, in that scenario – this character actor becomes the star of the movie.'

Some examples are Om Prakash in *Chupke Chupke*, Pran in *Zanjeer*; Sanjeev Kumar in *Khilona*, Madan Puri in *Dulhan Wohi Jo Piya Man Bhaye* and *Upkar* and *Purab aur Paschim* and Amrish Puri in most of his movies. Essentially, the character actor is the simple glue that binds all shows.

Villains are the characters, in drama and melodrama, that incarnate evil and work against the hero. Shakuni Mama was one of the pivotal

With Hiralal and Sham Lal

With Ranjeeta in *Akhiyon Ke Jharokon Se* (1978)

With Anwar and David

With Ajit in *Ali Baba aur Chalis Chor* (1980)

*Waqt* (1965)

With Shyama and David

With Amitabh Bachchan
in *Zameer* (1975)

With Amitabh Bachchan and Vinod Khanna in *Ittefaq* (1969)

With Jeevan
in *Angaray*
(1977)

In *Ek Paheli* (1971)

With Prem
Chopra,
Kamini
Kaushal,
Manoj
Kumar and
Kanhaiya
Lal in
*Upkaar*
(1967)

*Zameer* (1975)

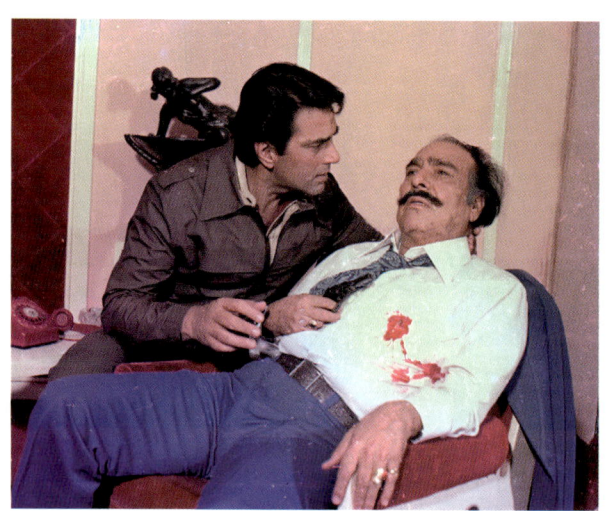

With Dharamendra in
*The Burning Train* (1980)

In *Sharada* (1981)

With Manoj Kumar in *Yaadgaar* (1970)

With Dina Pathak in *Sautela Pati* (1986)

players in the Mahabharata. For villains, all paths are wide open. Perhaps the nefarious acts of well-delineated villains make some people identify with them as characters more strongly than they do with the heroes. They help us to mentally fulfill our fantasies.

K N Singh Saab lived in our locality and once, when I was young and brash, I said to him Uncle, why do you make all those frightening faces in the movies and you never laugh the way you do at home? He gave me one of his trade mark sinister looks and then smilingly said that in the era before sound in movies, villains had to appear very 'visually sinister', and thus many villain stereotypes were born. The villains had dens and gambling houses and molls and hordes of henchmen hanging around. These stereotypes include black clothing (often quite formal – capes, top hats, etc), facial hair, sharp features, and a perpetually 'angry' facial expression. There is an opposing stereotype of the suave and polished villains like Motilal, Pran and Madan Puri who look like heroes, but their personality and attitudes betray a diabolical nature. Another stereotype was villains from the rural area like Jeevan and Kanhaiya Lal. Kanhaiya Lal was a great artiste who never achieved his full potential. His acting in *Upkaar* was outstanding. His performance in *Mother India* would even today be incomparable.

Siddharth Bhatia, author and film critic says: 'Wong was the most popular name for a Chinese film villain in Hindi cinema and more often than not, was played by the veteran character actor Madan Puri. His first Wong was in *Howrah Bridge*, where he was a Kolkata Chinaman criminal. But in at least two films, *Shatranj* and *Prem Pujari*, his Wong was a member of the Chinese secret service. Puri, a versatile actor who could play a thug, a gangland boss or the kindly uncle with equal flair, took to the Chinese persona with great felicity and he was a must-have in spy films.' (*Time Out*, 16 March 2012).

Bauji always said that it was more fun playing the villain than the hero. The hero had to look good and whisper sweet nothings to the heroine while the villain had to play his role so convincingly that the audience began to hate him. Every abuse hurled at the villain was a compliment to the artiste.

It was a very happy day for Bauji when V Shantaram signed him to play Madan Babu, the suave and polished villain in *Jhanak Jhanak Paayal Baaje* (1956). He felt that he had been finally accepted in the industry.

The most important of Bauji's professional ethics entailed that seniors receive due respect. He cited the Kapoor family as a shining example of correct protocol.

Bauji practiced what he preached. Our grandfather passed away in 1976 at the age of ninety-three. The day after the rituals, Bauji suggested that Chaman tayaji and Amrish chachaji should go to work, and he would do the same. He said, 'The loss is ours, why should the producer suffer?'

On one occasion Bauji was told that a popular but arrogant hero was bad-mouthing him. Bauji asked the actor if the story was true, and if so would he like to apologise so the matter could be closed. The actor repeated his words with even more arrogance. Bauji publicly slapped the actor, who then threatened police and legal action. However, all those present told the hero that he was at fault and nobody would give evidence against Madanji. He was advised to apologise, which he finally did, and the matter was closed.

Bauji never had a secretary or a press agent. He carried a diary to note his shooting dates and changes, if any. In this way there was no confusion or misunderstanding. On some days he would be working at two or three locations, in fact, during the shooting of *Upkaar* (1967) he was working at Bombay, Gurgaon and Madras simultaneously for a fortnight.

Ramnesh was witness to one of his principles. Bauji was sitting on his carpet, shaving, when a producer and his director came to meet him with a movie offer. After some discussion Bauji quoted a very high figure. They said that they would revert, and left.

An hour later another producer walked in and surprisingly, Bauji told him that he would accept whatever was offered. The producer quoted a small sum and then left some money as a signing amount. Ramnesh asked why there was such a disparity between the two quotes. Bauji said that the producer had been in the industry for a long time but did not have much finance, so Bauji was prepared to work for him at any price. A few days later they had a *mahurat* at Essel Studios. Bauji spent the entire signing amount on arranging drinks and dinner for the unit. Sadly, the movie was never completed. As for the other producer, Bauji did not wish to be associated with him.

Once in the early sixties we were sitting on the carpet, when a gentleman walked in. After a few pleasantries, he asked Bauji for a loan of a few thousands. I got up to leave the room, but Bauji signaled me to sit down. Bauji gave him ₹ 500, and told him that this was the last time that he should ask for money as he had never returned previous loans. Later, Bauji told me that the visitor used be a great star but had squandered all his money. Because of his profligate habits he had no work and was reduced to begging. Bauji always advised that one should never take a loan (he never took a loan in all his life), and if you need to give one, offer a small amount and then mentally write it off as a gift. If you demand it back, then invariably you have lost your money as well as a friend.

Bauji loved to meet his fans. Once while he was on a visit to London for a premiere a large group of fans mobbed the team. The hero complained loudly that the fans did not leave them alone. Bauji suggested that he should enjoy the adulation while it lasted, saying, 'Once your popularity wanes you will feel very miserable when nobody recognises you.'

One Holi, Bauji and Ramnesh were returning home when they were stopped by a large group of revellers near Plaza Cinema. Bauji immediately came out of the car and joined them in their revelry. He always said that fans would never hurt him; they showed their appreciation of his acting ability when they forgot the difference between the actor's real persona and his film role. He had learnt this from Dev Anand, who always mixed with the public, saying that nobody would ever harm the artistes.

If a producer rang to say that his shooting schedule had been cancelled, Bauji would call up the other producers to inform them that he was free. By the grace of God, he had so much work that he could always go to another shoot. That may have been one of the reasons why he was much in demand. We criticised Bauji for working for the same producers again and again when most of them didn't pay him much and others paid him less than the agreed amount. He said, 'What is my investment in this business? I have an acceptable face and some talent. If I don't receive the full amount, how does it matter? Besides, the producer has not rejected my demand. He has only said, Puri Saab, I shall pay you later. In the process, I have made a friend, and when he starts the next movie, he will remember my cooperation. This is how my business continues to flourish. The public goes to see a movie because of the hero and heroine, and sometimes it is the reputation of the director, or the music. Nobody goes to see a movie just because Madan Puri is acting in it. One must know his marketability and demand accordingly.'

This realistic policy paid Bauji good dividends. He was a popular actor, and in the seventies he was one of the busiest in Bombay. At one time he had twenty-two movies on the sets, while his good friend Shatrughan Sinha had twenty-seven. In the industry the saying was that if you want to make a movie, then all that you need is an Arriflex camera, some raw stock and Madan Puri.

Madan Puri never asked for a separate make up room. He did not feel bad about waiting between shots. He enjoyed company. Most actors were genuinely fond of him and his sense of repartee and candid observations made him an absolute delight to be with.

He would say, 'I am a husband and a father and an actor but I have never allowed any of my actions to adversely affect any of these responsibilities. I have been able to create compartments and one compartment can only impinge on another if I say so. The moment I enter my home, it is Madan Puri, family man. When I step out to work, it is Madan Puri, film actor.'

Bauji enjoyed working for producers from the South and admired their work ethic and discipline. He was also very happy with their system of making payments on schedule. Every time he returned from Madras, he would have spent the money he had received on gifts for all.

Bauji was a totally dedicated and committed actor with a positive attitude, who loved his work and enjoyed every moment of it. He worked only for those he knew and liked. Before accepting an assignment, he wanted to hear his role, and would agree to work only if he had faith in the director.

Bauji was a good storyteller, and understood screenplay and the importance of correct characterisation. He was a keen observer, and people he knew or had seen were the inspiration for many of the characters he portrayed. He always gave credit for characterisation to his writers and the director. He was not a 'method' actor, but immersed himself in the character he was playing in order to give a performance that the audience would find credible. Although many of his roles depicted reprehensible human beings, he worked hard to understand them.

As a rule, once Bauji came on the set he stayed on after his own shot was over to watch the other actors perform, because he said it helped him in improving his performance. He never tried to advise or teach a co-artiste unless they requested guidance, because he felt that 'acting is reacting' and maybe that was the way the other actor felt. He practiced what he preached, never took anything for granted, and never let anybody take him for granted. He hated the '*ho jayega yaar*' attitude. He never exploited his position in anyway, nor did he allow the producers to exploit any artiste or technician.

When *Aradhana* was almost complete, Burman Dada decided to add another song, *Safal hogi teri aradhana,* and he planned to sing it himself. One of Shakti Saab's greatest qualities was his willingness to listen to advice and then decide for himself. The song was being composed at Burman Dada's house; Ramnesh as an Assistant Director was present because Shakti Saab wanted some changes in the tune. Bauji was a good friend of Burman Dada. He had asked Bauji to drop in to provide some moral support. Burman Dada sang and Bauji exclaimed, '*Wah*!' Dada instantly stopped singing and asked, 'Who said *Wah*?' Everybody was taken aback, thinking that Dada was offended. But Dada gave a big smile and told Shakti Saab, '*Agar yeh Aurangzeb ko bhi gana acha laga to Saab yeh tune change nahin hoga… aare yeh Puri Saab jo sa re ga nahin gaa sakta hai, usne* prove *kiya ki* woh *apna kaan se* music *samajta hai…*' Burman Dada did not change the tune and the song was recorded the very next day.

Once, Bauji, Beeji and Ramnesh were going to Malad to Chaman tayaji's house, and they stopped at Asif Studios en route. Bauji called Ramnesh to meet Mr K. Asif, the maker of *Mughal-e-Azam*, one of the highest grossers of its time. By the time the movie was completed Asif Saab was deeply in debt. While they were still there some members of his staff spoke to Asif Saab, and he gave them instructions. As they left, the staff members returned carrying a carpet. Later, Bauji remarked that they had come for their dues, but this great man had no money. So he told them to take the carpet from his office, and sell it off to recover their money. That was K Asif!

Madan Puri's lasting contribution to the film industry was the setting up of the Character Artistes Association, along with stalwarts like Manmohan Krishna, Prithvi Raj Kapoor, Pran, Jayant and many others. During the fifties and sixties the industry was doing well but the benefits went mostly to the producers, the financiers and the top stars. The rest had a rough time, especially junior technicians, junior artistes (then called 'extras') and other assistants. Manmohan Krishna and Bauji had not forgotten their own difficult days and were very concerned. Many discussions took place, mostly at their residences, and from these discussions the Character Artists

Association was born. The CAA spawned sixteen other workers' unions and brought some discipline into the working conditions of the film industry.

The first meeting of the CAA was held at Shree Sound Studios on 17 March 1958. The Association was registered under the Indian Trade Union Act (1958). The same day, at a meeting held with Mr J B Roongta, President IMPPA, the Association was generously given offices at Famous Studios, Mahalakshmi, at half the rentals.

The definition of a character actor was: 'A character actor is one who has been billed as a star or a featured player and has played various types of roles in films.'

The CAA became a very powerful voice for the workers. The Federation of Associations was able to call and sustain a strike for over a month against the producers.

On 18 August 1960 the name of the Association was changed to Cine Artistes Association. It is a matter of pride that Chaman Puri was Treasurer for many years and was also the Vice President. Madan Puri was the Founder-Treasurer, and later the President in 1983. Amrish Puri was the President from 2000 until his death in January 2005.

## THE LAST OUTDOOR

Bauji had worked with Raj Kumar Kohli in seven movies and they shared a great rapport. He had not finished his work for *Saazish* when he began wasting away in mid-1984, but he told Kohli Saab to go ahead and make the arrangements. The shooting was in the lobby of a Singapore hotel, and my parents were put up in the same hotel. He had by now lost over thirty kilos. The makeup artist put rubber padding inside his cheeks and air pillows inside his coat to create the illusion of a dynamic man. When the shot was ready, my mother was informed. They would take the elevator to the lobby, give the shot and go back, totally exhausted, till the camera was ready again. That was the man's commitment to his work.

## LAST DUBBING

The last dubbing that Bauji did was for B R Ishara's *Sautela Pati*, which was released after his demise. By mid-1984, cancer had a tight grip on him. The producer had become impatient as shooting was held up due to his illness. Bauji ordered Ramnesh to take him to the dubbing studio. Ramnesh carried him into the studio, and after a few shots the producer realised that Madanji was indeed very ill. Bauji was always very concerned about the moviemaker, and felt the producer should never have to suffer because of Madan Puri's problems. He completed all his professional commitments before the end.

## LAST SHOOTING

Bauji's last shooting was for Gulshan Rai's '*Yudh*'. From the shots it is painfully obvious that he was desperately ill. One can see his co-artists supporting him and helping him to stand.

Yash Chopra, with whom Bauji had a great relationship, came to meet him in the hospital a few days before his death. Bauji had been hospitalised for nearly a year and expenses had been heavy. While leaving, Mr Chopra gave him a packet of money and said that this was an advance for the next movie. Bauji smiled, thanked Yashji and returned the packet. 'When I am recovered,' he said, 'I shall come and report on duty and then I shall take the advance… but thank you for the thought.'

Madan Puri compared with the best character actors of the classical era such as Prithviraj Kapoor, Motilal, Jayant, Pran, Om Prakash and many others. He could create a character that was villainous or sympathetic, authoritative or pitiful, by making slight adjustments to his gaze, posture, walk, and diction. He was never typecast. In one movie he played the combination of villain and comedian. His villain was a monster and his positive roles were endearing.

Madan Puri had a vast histrionic range, he coached himself by observing people. I recollect one particular incident in the late sixties, when we had a death in the family and we were all heartbroken. I did not wish to display my emotions so I went to the side of the hospital building and wept some silent tears. Bauji noticed my absence and came looking for me. That memory stayed in his mind, and he used it to telling effect in Yash Chopra's *Noorie*. His daughter is pining for her lover and he cannot bear to see her sorrow, so he goes to the side of the hut and weeps piteously.

Whenever he visited my army stations he would watch my colleagues and me and carry some of the mannerisms back in his mind.

Madan Puri's career went through three phases; each had his unique stamp of originality. There was considerable overlap between the villain and the good guy, which showed the versatility of the man who could play all kinds of roles with consummate artistry.

He came into movies in 1945 in Bombay as a hero. Some of his movies were *Kuldeep* (1946), *Imtehaan* (1946), *Santosh* (1947), *Capt Nirmala* (1947) and *Sona* (1948). He did not have much success, until he decided to switch to supporting actor roles.

The second phase was as a villain, at which he excelled. He played the villain in three movies, one after another, namely *Vidya* (1948), *Namoona* (1949) and *Jeet* (1949). His work was highly appreciated and he carved a niche for himself as the iconic villain. Some other noteworthy performances during this period were *Goonj* (1951) and *Jhanak Jhanak Payal Baaje* (1955), where he performed an iconic caricature dance. His work was much liked and he felt that he had broken into the big league when V Shantaram, a very discerning director, gave him an important role. Another good performance was in *Sheroo* (1957) opposite Ashok Kumar, who appreciated his rugged style of acting.

His performance in *Howrah Bridge* (1958) earned him many accolades. One filmgoer commented, 'Madan Puri comes out with a rare piece of histrionic talent in this film. As the mysterious Chinese hotel owner Wong, he has proved his versatility, giving a very convincing performance.'

*Howrah Bridge* was closely followed by *Kala Bazaar* (1960), which made the industry sit up and take note. A comment made by a noted film person was, 'After seeing *Kala Bazaar* I am in a mood to hand out bouquets and my first bouquet must positively go to MADAN PURI for the most outstanding performance in the entire cast of one dozen seasoned artistes. I have seen him and watched him, but he was never so brilliant as when he portrayed Ganesh Dada, the Bully whose sinews were made of steel. But, even steel is pliant and it melts before the spiritual greatness of Dev Anand.'

His Bad Man (sic) roles continued with movies like *Waqt* (1965) and *Shagird* (1967).

The third phase was when he started playing the good guy. By this time he was in his fifties and not getting any younger. Running around trees chasing nubile beauties was definitely not good for his knees and his heart. Besides, he was already a grandfather and not everybody can brazen it out like Dev Anand. Over time his roles mostly moved away from villainy and concentrated on senior 'good guy' roles, for which he is best remembered.

*Aradhana* (1970) was a positive role well played. He had the role of a jailor who retires on the same day that Sharmila Tagore finishes her jail term for murder. He offers to take her home as his sister. There was pin drop silence in the hall when he made the offer and she accepted. The audience was left wondering what new difficulties she would now have to face. However he played his role to perfection.

Another great performance came in *Purab Paschim* (1970). He plays Saira Banu's father. He has settled in London but pines for his *watan* and its values. At the club, he watches his daughter Saira Banu having a drink and a smoke. At this moment while KL Saigal's song '*Babul mora nahiar chootath jaye*' was being played, Madan Puri wipes away a tear with a wistful look. It was a great directorial touch by Manoj Kumar.

Madan Puri had a flair for comedy and he displayed it in many movies like *Blackmail* (1973). This Vijay Anand directed thriller had

Madan Puri playing a scientist who makes revolutionary discoveries. His comic timing was perfect.

Shakti Films' *Anuraag* (1972) was an intense emotional drama in which Madan Puri played father to Vinod Mehra. It was the story of a young boy who has leukemia at the age of ten. Before his death he donates his eyes to Moushami Chatterjee, a blind orphan. Madan Puri's performance was in a comical vein, and it so impressed Tarachand Baratjya of Rajshri Productions that he decided to cast him as the father in *Geet Gaata Chal* and as the grandfather in *Dulhan Wohi Jo Piya Man Bhaiye*

*Geet Gata Chal* (1975) was one more outstanding film from the Rajshri banner. Madan Puri shows his versatility in playing the role of a Colonel whose son, an Army captain, dies in action. The Colonel keeps pretending that he is still alive and cannot come home due to official commitments. He continues to celebrate his son's birthday every year and he even has to do a song and dance sequence, which he carries off with aplomb.

*Apna Desh* (1975). The big starrer from the South had him looking as debonair as ever. The cast of villains included Om Prakash, Kanhaiya Lal and Sunder. Rajesh Khanna and Mumtaz were the leading couple.

*Fakira* (1976). This N N Sippy Production had him playing the villain, Chiman Lal, with gusto and indulging in rape, loot and terror. He also gave a very good performance as a comedian. His mannerisms in the comedy situations were superb.

*Dulhan Wohi Jo Piya Man Bhaye* (1977). There could not have been a more natural grandfather than Madan Puri. It was his movie and Lekh Tandon had judged his potential well. The general opinion was that while the hero and heroine performed well yet the best performance in the movie was that of Madan Puri. He held the audience from the beginning to the end of the movie. He was perhaps the most suitable actor for this role. Shatrughan Sinha had expressed similar sentiments when I interviewed him.

*Akhiyon ke Jharokon Se* (1978). This was a very tender romance, which ends tragically. Sachin and Sarika played college mates from different social standings. Madan Puri, the understanding father tells Sachin to go ahead and marry his love. Fate plays a very cruel trick and Sarika dies of leukemia. Madan Puri's performance was much appreciated.

*Lok Parlok* (1979) gave Madan Puri ample scope to display his histrionics. He played the villain. He was the evil zamindar, Kallicharan, and yet he played it in a comic way.

*Prem Geet* (1981). This Raj Babbar – Anita Raj movie had Madan Puri playing father to Raj Babbar and father-in-law to Anita Raj. His handling of the couple's complex relationship and his emotional responses to the unfolding situations showed the depth and maturity of Madan Puri's histrionics.

*Kranti* (1981). Sivaji Ganesan in his autobiography had said that there is no such thing as a big or a small role. If an actor is good, he will shine. Madan Puri proved this in *Kranti*. There was actually no role for him, but Manoj Kumar gave him a two-line dialogue and asked him to work on it. Atal Bihari Vajpayee favourably commented upon his performance at a special showing and so did Masoom Ali Raza who said that the movie was very good but the best performance was that of Madan Puri.

These are a few comments on the more than four hundred movies that he acted in over forty years. The transformation from villain to character actor that had started with *Aradhana* (1970) and *Purab aur Paschim* (1970) was now in full flower with *Geet Gata Chal* (1975), *Dulhan Wohi Jo Piya Man Bhaye* (1977) and *Prem Geet* (1981).

In 1952, Ashok Kumar had complimented Madan Puri on their first shooting together, saying, 'Madan Puri, you have a great sense of timing.' That prediction was repeatedly confirmed.

It is *Aloo-Pyaaz* like this that makes the curry memorable.

# 17 | BAUJI'S COLLEAGUES

## DILIP KUMAR

Dilip Kumar and Madan Puri first met at the Mohan Studios, Andheri, in 1957. Dilip Saab was playing cricket with the studio workers. He hit the ball and Madan Puri took the catch in passing. Dilip Saab declared himself out, and, intrigued by the handsome stranger, took him to his office and later to his house.

Their first movie together was *Dastaan*. Madan Puri arrived late on the sets for the *mahurat* shot. He apologised for the delay, and hastened to explain that he was normally very punctual but had been held up in traffic.

Dilip Saab said that Madan Puri was not late; he had already given one shot! Bauji was nonplussed. Dilip Saab explained that it was a long shot and he had worn Bauji's costume and given the shot to save time. Bauji often said that it was a singular honour that Dilip Kumar had worked as his 'double' (this incident is also recorded in Dilip Kumar's autobiography).

He always said, 'Dilip Kumar is a great star. He is also a great man and is always polite and well mannered. He is well read and can discourse on any subject. He has a phenomenal memory and recollects events of many years past with great accuracy. I consider myself fortunate to have known him.' They worked together in six movies: *Daastan* (1972), *Bairaag* (1976), *Kranti* (1981), *Vidhaata* (1982), *Mazdoor* (1983), *Mashaal* (1984).

Tom Alter told me a wonderful anecdote about the shooting of *Vidhaata*. In a scene on the beach, Dilip Kumar was confronted by Madan Puri and six of his henchmen. Dilip Kumar, being a perfectionist, took a dozen retakes. Madanji decided to liven up the proceedings and loudly said, '*Arre yaar, Yusuf, mere samne* nervous *mat hona*.' Everybody burst out laughing, Dilip Saab hugged Madanji and the shot was taken.

## SHAMMI KAPOOR

Bauji always called Shammi by his pet name 'Shamriya' and Shammi would call him Maddi Puttar. Shammi Saab said, 'We had some good times during the outdoor shoots of *Evening in Paris*. Madan uncle affectionately gave my daughter-in-law *shagun* when he met her for the first time. He was a contented man who earned the respect of the film fraternity.'

He and Bauji worked together in *Mirza Saheban* (1957), *Singapore* (1960), *China Town* (1962), *Kashmir ki Kali* (1964), *Evening in Paris* (1966), *Tumse Acha Kaun Hai* (1969), *Manoranjan* (1974), *Vidhaata* (1982), *Baadal* (1985).

I met Shammi Kapoor and his wife Neela at their home on Malabar Hill in 2009. I was warmly received, entertained and they both came out to see me to my car.

Shammi Kapoor joined Bauji on 14 August 2011, and they must be having *Manoranjan* in heaven!

## RANDHIR KAPOOR

I met Randhir Kapoor at his beautiful office at RK Studios. The place just breathes Raj Kapoor.

Randhir said, 'Raj Kapoor used to call him Madan uncle, so for me he was like a great-uncle. I had tremendous love and regard for him. Madan uncle used to say, 'We are colleagues and you are my friend, and that is the way in which we must maintain our professional relationship. It is only in a friendly environment that we can give our best performance.'"

'He was one of the few actors that I really enjoyed working with. He was friendly with everybody and gave advice only when it was asked for. On his own he would never interfere with anybody's work. When newcomers became stars and moved into a higher orbit, he never felt bad or commented on it.'

'One day I was smoking on the sets when Madan uncle walked in; out of respect I threw my cigarette away. He noticed this and said, "Please carry on smoking!"'

'He once told me that movies run on the stars and the producers. The rest of the cast is only required to fill in the blanks. We are like the *aloo-pyaaz* that can be put into any dish. I am aware that for every role that I audition, there are at least twenty equally versatile actors standing in line. Good behaviour is very important. A director can tolerate a bad actor but he cannot tolerate an indisciplined actor. He was always very cooperative and congenial.'

Bauji and Randhir worked together in eight movies: *Ponga Pandit* (1975), *Dafaa 302* (1975), *Khalifa* (1976), *Bhanwaar* (1976), *Ram Bharose* (1977), *HeeraLal PannaLal* (1978), *Humse Na Jeeta Koi* (1983), *Khazana* (1984).

# RISHI KAPOOR

Rishi Kapoor remembered Bauji with great fondness. 'My first movie with Madan uncle was *Zahreela Insaan. Bobby* had catapulted me into super-stardom and there had been no time to learn the fine art of acting in depth. I was quite tense to be working with Madan uncle and to make matters worse it was a fight scene. I landed a very hard blow on his lower lip. It started bleeding profusely and he lost his temper and berated me for not doing the shot with customary care. He was very angry and I was very scared. After some time he explained to me how such fight shots are to be handled. We worked together again in *Rafoo Chakkar*.'

'Madan uncle always said acting was an art that had to be learnt. He was fun to work with. He had no ego trips. Everybody said that he was a great actor and even more important he was a great human being.'

'I remember we worked together in Bhappie Soni's *Bade Dilwale* and we had gone to Shimla for the shoot. Roopesh Kumar, Madanji and I traveled together on the return trip. At Solan, Madanji went into a small vegetable shop, hugged the shabbily dressed owner, and introduced him to us as his old schoolmate. He gave him a small gift and then with tears in his eyes he said goodbye. We then drove to Chandigarh, where we dropped in to meet Madanji's son, Lt Col K K Puri.'

Rishi and Bauji worked together in seven movies: *Zahreela Insaan* (1974), *Rafoo Chakkar* (1975), *Barood* (1976), *Naya Daur* (1978), *Dhan Daulat* (1980), *Naukar Biwi Ka* (1983), *Bade Dil Wale* (1983).

## NEETU SINGH

Rishi's wife Neetu Singh had also worked with Bauji, and said that she had been very fond of Madan uncle, and had great regard for him as a man and for his talent. She called Madan Puri as 'Madi uncle' and Rajesh Khanna called him 'Unclino'.

Bauji and Neetu Singh worked together in eleven movies: *Aina* (1974), *Insaan* (1974), *Rafoo Chakkar* (1975), Deewar (1975), *Heeralal Pannalal* (1976), *Aatish* (1979) *Jaani Dushman* (1979), *The Great Gambler* (1979), *Kaala Pathar* (1979), *Dhan Daulat* (1980), *The Burning Train* (1980).

## PREM CHOPRA

I had a wonderful meeting with Prem Chopra at the Sun–n–Sand, Juhu, on 3 April 2009. We spoke for a long time, and I could tell from the emotion in his voice that he missed my father.

*Dr Vidya* was one of their first movies together. 'Madanji was very considerate towards newcomers and was willing to guide them if they wished. He was a very fine actor; each performance was different from the last. He was sincere and hard working, well read and had a good knowledge of Urdu poetry. His love and concern for his colleagues led him to become a founder member of the Cine Artistes Association.'

'On one occasion he played a practical joke on one of his colleagues. They were at an outdoor shooting and Madanji and another actor were flirting around with the heroine's mother. Late in the night, Madanji called up the actor in his hotel room and in a threatening voice he said "*Dekho, main Madan Puri hoon aur bahut khatarnakh aadmi hoon. Maine abhi tak karib 10 aadmiyon ka khoon kar diya hai, to agar tumhe aapni jaan pyaari hai to meri jaan se door raho*." From the next day the colleague stayed a mile away from the heroine's mother.'

The thirty-six movies in which Prem Chopra and Madan Puri worked together were: *Chowdhary Karnail Singh* (1960*), Dr Vidya* (1962*), Shaheed* (1965), *Upkar* (1967), *Aamne Saamne* (1967), *Hai Mera Dil* (1968), *Duniya* (1968), *Prem Pujari* (1970), *Kati Patang* (1970), *Yaadgaar* (1970), *Purab Paschim* (1970), *Hulchul* (1971), *Shor* (1972), *Dastaan* (1972), *Apraadh* (1972), *Gora aur Kaala* (1972), *Qeemat* (1973), *Nafrat* (1973), *Daag* (1973), *Ajnabee* (1974), *Jab Andhera Hota Hai* (1974), *Bairaag* (1976), *Mehbooba* (1976), *Barood* (1976), *Paapi* (1977), *Kaala Pathar* (1979), *Kasam Khoon Ki* (1977), *The Great Gambler* (1979), *Ali Baba aur Chalis Chor* (1980), *Dan Daulat* (1980), *Kranti* (1981), *Hathkadi* (1982), *Sawaal* (1982), *Andha Kanoon* (1983), *Awaaz (1984), Santosh (1985).*

## SHAKTI SAMANTHA

Madan Puri's 'Wong' in *Howrah Bridge* was an unforgettable cameo. When I asked Shakti Saab how he managed to extract such outstanding work from my father he said Madan Puri was a 'director's actor' because he surrendered himself totally to the director and to the character that he was portraying. 'Madan Puri had no ego problems about the role being small or big, important or insignificant. Every role was a different challenge, which is why he was not stereotyped in his performances. His work ethics were very strong. He was an easy man to get along with and all ages and social levels enjoyed his company.'

The shooting of *Insaan Jaag Utha* at Nagararjuna Sagar Dam was a time of bonding for Shakti Samantha, Sunil Dutt and Madan Puri. Drinking was taboo on the sets. After the day's work they would go for an evening swim at the dam. They each carried a bottle of beer, which was left to chill while they bathed, and then they would discuss the day's work and enjoy their beer. Shakti Saab passed away in April 2009 at the age of 83. It was a great loss for the film industry.

The twenty-two movies that Bauji acted in for Shakti Films were: *Howrah Bridge* (1958*), Insaan Jaag Utha* (1959), *Singapore* (1960*), Jaali Note* (1960), *China Town* (1962), *Naughty Boy* (1962), *Ek Raaz* (1963), *Kashmir Ki Kali* (1964), *Sawan Ki Ghata* (1966), *Evening in Paris* (1966), *Kati Patang* (1970), *Aradhana* (1970), *Amar Prem* (1971), *Anuraag* (1972), *Ajnabee* (1974), *Charitraheen* (1974), *Mehbooba* (1976*), The Great Gambler* (1979*), Khwaab* (1980*), Aayash* (1982*), Main Awara Hoon,* (1983), *Awaaz* (1984*).

## MANOJ KUMAR

Manoj Kumar considered Bauji to be more like a father than a colleague. He rang me up on Independence Day 2007 to say that he was watching *Shaheed* on TV, and invited me the next day to his residence.

Manoj said, 'I met Madan uncle for the first time at Ranjit Studio during the making of *Dr Vidya*. I was hesitant to smoke in the presence of a senior and I put out my cigarette. To put me at ease Madanji offered me a cigarette. In *Shaheed*, Madanji gave a marvellous performance as the Jailor. When we were shooting the hanging scene, I saw the intense look and the tremor of Madanji's lower lip as he looked at his watch. I took the entire scene in one shot. Madanji shed actual tears, as did most of the unit members.'

'In *Upkaar* he was shown snatching jewellery from the dead. I asked him to give an evil look into the camera. No *Kans Mama* could have been so vile! Madanji congratulated me and said, "*Tu toh Mehboob Khan ke muqabale ka director hai.* Well done. Keep it up."'

'Madan Puri was a devoted family man. In 1966, we were shooting at Gurgaon for *Upkaar* and Madanji made a request that he would like to go home for Diwali, as it was the first Diwali of his daughter-in-law. He was to return after a couple of days but he did not come in time. It seems that Nasir Hussain was making *Bahaaron Ke Sapne* and had managed to get a mill outdoors and so asked Madanji to please stay on for a couple of days. Madanji reluctantly agreed. When he returned, I initially refused his cigarette and the *batata wadas* (which I like very much) and which he had specially brought for me from Bombay.' The whole day there was tension and finally some senior colleagues like Pran and Manmohan Krishna suggested to Manoj Kumar that he should let bygones be bygones. That evening Manoj Saab requested Madan uncle for a cigarette and bonhomie was restored.

'Our mutual respect was cemented during the making of *Upkaar*. One day Madanji asked me, "Why are you so strict with yourself and your crew?"'

'I said, I have learnt from you to be disciplined and punctual. He was very happy that he had got a convert!'

'In *Kranti*, we felt unhappy that there was no suitable role for Madanji even though he was an integral part of our unit. A cameo role was created for him as Sher Singh, a jailer on board the ship carrying prisoners to *Kala Pani*. I gave Madanji two lines of dialogue and asked him to sketch out his role. The English captain (Tom Alter) brusquely orders Sher Singh to bring Hema Malini to his quarters. Sher Singh smiles slyly and rushes to do his bidding. Then the Captain abuses him and says, 'It is because of dogs like you that a handful of British are able to rule India.' Sher Singh suddenly realises that he is ill-treating his own countrymen, who are fighting for the country's Independence. Sher Singh stands in front of the mirror and says '*Sher Singh, tu sher ban kar to nahin jia, ab sher ban kar marna.*' Sher Singh throws away his uniform and tells the Captain that he will not work for the British any more. The Captain orders the crew to throw Sher Singh into the sea… When Madanji fell into the water, there were four stunt men waiting to retrieve him!'

'I had arranged a special showing of *Kranti* for Prime Minister Atal Bihari Vajyapee at Delhi. After the show the PM asked me to convey his special compliments to Madan Puri for a brilliant performance.'

'Madan uncle was entertaining, very disciplined, a man of tradition, and yet he embraced every reasonable new idea. His best quality was that he was a close member of the unit and mixed well with everybody, and they always looked forward to working with him again. Everybody enjoyed his professionalism and his wit. He never made fun of anybody; all his jokes were directed towards himself. He played all kinds of roles with equal ease. Most character actors have a fixed style or mannerism, but with Madanji each performance was unique. While we were working in *Gumnaam* (1965), I noticed that he wore the same set of clothes throughout the movie. I asked him why he did not have a larger wardrobe. His reply was that one set of clothes helps to fix the character in the eyes of the audience; they can then concentrate on his performance and not be dazzled by his outfits. I thought that it was a good idea and I adopted the same principle in *Dus Numbri.*'

'For *Purab Paschim*, I had originally planned to cast Balraj Sahni as Saira Banu's father. Balraj Saheb's staff could not work out the dates, etc, and his negotiator said nobody else would fit this role. I took up the challenge and asked Madanji for dates. My hunch proved right and I never regretted not getting Balraj Sahni for the part. In the restaurant scene, when Saigal's song *Naihar Chootath Jae* was being played, Madanji shed actual tears. I kept the camera on his face, and recorded a great performance. My staff and I took great care to ensure that all dress details were covered. Madanji, a perfectionist, pointed out that an Englishman never went anywhere without his brolly!'

'Balraj Sahni always used to pinch half a cigarette from me, but when we met after the release of the movie he took a full one, saying, "You have made a great movie and you have shown guts in giving such a pivotal role to a villain." Balraj Saab then rang up Madanji and said, "You were very good, even better than me." Madanji had been a great villain till *Upkaar*, but *Purab Paschim* gave him a role makeover, and he came to be accepted for positive roles as well.'

'Madanji was a close friend of my father's who always enjoyed his company and said that Madan Puri was a very cultured man. I learnt from Madanji that our children would only respect us if we gave respect to our elders.'

'On one occasion, I heard Madanji berating a fairly popular star. I asked him the reason. He said, 'this man is sitting in your house and bad-mouthing another top hero behind his back. I told him that if you have anything bad to say about somebody, say it to his face.'

'Madanji was a devoted family man and always tried to promote his younger brother Amrish Puri. When I was launching my younger son Kunal as a leading man, I was keen that Kunal should work under the guidance of Madanji, who, however, suggested that I try out Amrish Puri for the role. When Amrish Puri was contacted, he suggested that Madanji would be better suited for the role. This showed a good family tradition and strong upbringing.'

'Madanji was already unwell when we worked together in *Santosh*. Today he may not be present physically but I feel his presence all the time. He was an institution and institutions never die.'

Producer-Director Milan Luthria's uncle told me that Manoj Kumar had once arranged a special showing of *Kranti* for Masoom Ali Raza Saab, who commented that it was a good movie, the best part being Madan Puri's performance.

Madan Puri worked in seven movies produced by Manoj Kumar: *Shaheed* (1965), *Upkaar* (1967), *Saajan* (1969), *Purab aur Paschim*

(1970), *Shor* (1972), *Roti Kapda aur Makaan* (1974), *Kranti* (1981).

They also worked together in movies made by other producers: *Dr Vidya* (1962), *Gumnaam* (1965), *Saawan Ki Ghata* (1965), *Yaadgaar* (1970), *Purani Pehchan* (1970), *Shirdi ke Sai* (1977), *Jat Punjabi* (1979), *Santosh* (1984).

## B R CHOPRA

B R Chopra's first movie *Afsana* (1951) was a commercial success. His popularity started with *Naya Daur* (1957). He had a feel for socio-economic themes and made meaningful movies like *Dhool ka Phool*, *Gumrah* (1963), *Dhund* (1973), *Waqt* (1965) and many others. *Waqt* created a close bond between the Chopras and the Puris.

In 1969, Bauji was keen to buy a new car and got his Ambassador through the good offices of B R Films. The car arrived the same day that Kanchan was born and also established my close relationship with Yash Chopra. I would come on leave to Bombay for about two months every year. One day Yashji asked Bauji if his *fauji* son was on leave. Surprised, Bauji asked why? Yashji told him, 'Once or twice a year we get a bunch of parking tickets on the account of your car (the car was registered under B R Films) and now my staff tells me that there is a traffic violation ticket nearly every day.'

## YASH CHOPRA

I had phoned Yash Chopra to request a meeting to discuss my project. He said warmly that I was welcome any time, as Madanji was a favourite with everybody and his outgoing personality had generated many anecdotes. Cruel fate intervened. Before we could meet, Yash Rajji had joined my father. They must be sharing jokes and stories in heaven.

Yash Chopra established Yash Raj Films in 1973 and made movies with beautiful locales and glamorous lovers. Once on an outdoor shoot Yash Chopra was staying in the adjoining room and teased Madanji the next morning, saying that he had heard a girl moaning in ecstasy in Madanji's room. Bauji replied, 'Yash, will you vouch for this, and please tell everybody. It will enhance my youthful image.'

## RAVI CHOPRA

His beautifully appointed office at Santa Cruz (West) was the perfect setting for Ravi Chopra. Ravi told me, 'My first direct interaction with Madan uncle was in *Zameer*, when I was an assistant director. Madanji was a director's dream. He was a true character actor who could fit into any role whether it was negative or positive. He had a great feeling for the character that he played. He followed directions completely and only gave suggestions if asked. During the shooting for *Zameer* there was a scene on horseback with Shammi Kapoor and Madan Puri facing each other. Neither actor was comfortable on horseback. We arranged for some junior artistes to hold the horse's legs so that they did not take off with the actors! Madanji had to point towards Vinod Khanna and say: '*Yeh mera beta hai.*' He was so conscious of the horse that when he pointed towards Vinod Khanna he said, '*Yeh mera ghoda hai!*'

'The entire industry turned up for his funeral and we all felt an enormous sense of loss at the passing away of a great friend, a great human being and a great artiste.'

## SHATRUGHAN SINHA

It was a good feeling when Shatrughan Sinha called to acknowledge my request for a meeting. At his Lokhandwala house I was warmly received by his wife Poonam, elegant in a white salwar kameez, with a huge bindi and the parting of her hair lined with sindoor. While we were talking, their two sons, Luv and Kush, walked in and shook hands. Good breeding and culture shone through. Their daughter Sonakshi has emerged as a star.

Mr Sinha said, 'Madanji was a great human being and I was really blessed to have been his friend and confidante. He had a wonderful sense of humour and was always playful on the sets without losing his professional focus. He considered his work to be a great adventure. Madanji had a perfect sense of timing. He was more concerned about the strength of a role than the length. If it was small, he embellished it. In a Subhash Ghai movie, the phone rang. Madanji played it as comedy. He cupped his hand to his ear and kept on saying Hullo, Hullo, and then realised that the phone was lying beside him. His reactions were fantastic. A case in point was his role in *Kranti,* a small role of little significance, and yet it became one of the highlights of the movie. Madanji always made his presence felt.

'Once a moviemaker from Tamil Nadu was watching one of Madanji's movies and said, "I have been seeing his movies for many years, and yet he never ages!"'

Regarding the relevance of character actors when our movies are mostly star-driven, Mr Sinha said that if the character actor is good then he makes an impact like a star. In *Dulhan Wahi Jo Piya Man Bhaye* Madan Puri made a bigger impact than the star couple.

'He was part of the group of old timers like Yakub, Gope, Johnny Walker, Mehmood, Kanhaiya Lal, Jeevan, Nana Palsikar and others,' Mr Sinha said. 'They were indispensable and we miss them. The old saying is, "The show must go on". That is true, but the show is weakened by their absence. They were amongst the last of the Moghuls. We spent many pleasant hours in the makeup room between shots. There was laughter and happiness. Madan Puri was a person worth emulating and I miss him.'

Shatrughan Sinha and my father worked together in eighteen movies: *Saajan* (1969), *Prem Pujari* (1970), *Paras* (1971), *Blackmail* (1973), *Ek Naari Do Roop* (1973), *Kaali Charan* (1976), *Shirdi Ke*

*Sai* (1977), *Chor Ho to Aisa* (1978), *Vishwanath* (1978), *Muqabala* (1979), *Jaani Dushman* (1979), *Gautam Govinda* (1979), *Tere Pyaar Mein* (1979), *Kaala Pathar* (1979*)*, *Kranti* (1981), *Hathkaadi* (1982), *Badle Ki Aag* (1982), *Aaj Ka MLA Ram Avtar* (1984).

## CHANDRA SHEKHAR

Chandra Shekhar is an amazing man. His drive and determination is worthy of emulation. He joined films in 1941 as a junior artiste and then went on to become a character actor, hero, writer, producer and director. He also became a trade unionist to help improve the working conditions of the film fraternity. He said, 'Madanji was a great friend, who had carved a niche for himself as a character actor. He was a rare individual who had totally merged into the system and was comfortable at all levels of the film world.'

He reflected on the old days when music was melody; today it is mostly noise. He said that the film industry is like a *Vishwa Vidyalaya*. It teaches you everything about film-making, and one has the opportunity to do what he wants and achieve what he desires.

Chandra Shekhar directed and produced two movies, *Cha Cha Cha* (1964) and *Street Singer* (1966). Madan Puri acted in both these movies.

The government had started the system of annuities whereby the producer deposited a lump sum with LIC, and LIC paid out the amount to the actor in fixed instalments over an extended period. This reduced the tax burden on the actor and also ensured that the actor had some income when his movie career stopped. The government discontinued this system in 1980. Chandra Shekhar, Rekha and Shashi Kapoor accompanied the delegation that made a presentation to Mr Shankar Dayal Sharma, and Mr P Rama Rao, chairman of the Estimates Committee. They immediately reinstated the annuity system. My mother received these annuities for nearly twenty years after Bauji passed away.

# LEKH TANDON

Lekh Tandon said, 'My first big break in films as a director came with Rajshree's *Dulhan Wohi Jo Piya Man Bhaye*. I informed Madan chachaji and he was thrilled for my sake. Mr Tarachand Barjatya had seen Madan chachaji in *Anuraag*, and thought he would be perfect for the role of Dadaji. I then requested him to take the role. Madan chachaji objected, saying that I was casting him in a positive role, which the audience would never accept, and the movie would fail. However, as I was clear in my mind that Madan Puri was my man he finally agreed. Barjatya Saab proved to be right; Bauji went on to give one of the best performances of his career. *Dulhan Wohi Jo Piya Man Bhaaye* was a watershed movie for Madan Puri, as his transformation from the Bad Man of *Howrah Bridge* and *Upkaar* to the Good Guy of *Purab Paschim* was complete.

'After the success of *Dulhan Wohi Jo Piya Man Bhaye*, Madan chachaji suggested that I should buy a car, and in case finance was a problem then I could take his car and pay whenever able.'

'Madan Puri was a professional. He took great pains to prepare for his shots and he placed himself in the hands of the director. He had no *nakhras*, no demands and no attitude. He was a director's dream. He understood the role immediately and never took offence if the director was a little abrupt. Madan chachaji said that money was essential, but basically he loved to work. He was always at the centre of any merriment on the sets. He was very sporting and took all comments in good spirit.'

'Sometimes, some high profile stars insist on having their favourites to act with them. Others have actors that they would prefer not to work with. I cannot recollect a single star that preferred not to work with Puri Saab. He never permitted backbiting on the sets. Madanji was never involved in any controversy in this controversial industry. He generated no tension and was himself very relaxed.'

Lekh Saab then spoke about *Ek Baar Kaho,* starring Shabana Azmi and Anil Kapoor. They went to Kalimpong for the outdoor shoot. 'Madanji was very popular with the locals and specially the children. He was very fond of sweets, and we would regularly visit a mithaiwala for barfi. Madanji gave him some tips to improve his *barfi,* and even today there is a 'Madan Puri' barfi sold in Kalimpong.

'Madanji hated dubbing. He said it ruined the spontaneity of the words. Perhaps a stage artiste at heart, he liked to deliver the lines and see the audience respond immediately. I felt that Madanji was a great asset to any production unit; he was willing to accommodate the producers for dates even at short notice. Every role gave him a chance to showcase his abilities, and he was never bothered about the size. I miss him and his guidance and affection.'

## RAMESHWARI

I met Rameshhwari and her husband Deepak Seth at their Bandra residence. She said that the warmth, affection and encouragement that Madanji gave to younger artistes was amazing. She was very nervous when she came on the sets for the first time, but the moment she met Madan chachaji it was instant bonding like a *janam janam ka rishta*. Madan chachaji took her under his wing and guided her through the movie.

## TOM ALTER

In August 2006, Jane Bhandari invited me to a poetry evening organized by her at the Art and Soul Studio at Worli, part of an exhibition (curated by Himanshu Verma) called 'Monsoon Madness'. Tom Alter was one of the poets reading that evening. Jane introduced me to him with a brief reference to my parentage. When Tom heard the name Madan Puri, he became very emotional and said that Madanji was one of his icons. We decided to meet again to swap anecdotes.

Tom was a busy man, and it was almost a year before we could meet. On 16 July 2007, he came home for dinner, and we spent the evening remembering Madan Puri. There was much laughter and nostalgia as Tom shared his memories of my father.

Tom felt that Madan Puri was a man to be remembered and emulated, and suggested that I should write about him. That was my first nudge towards writing about my father. Feeling that time was running out, I immediately began making lists of my father's colleagues to interview.

*Ram Bharose*, made by Anand Sagar, was Tom's first movie, and he worked with Bauji. At the shooting of *Vidhaata*, produced by Subhash Ghai, Bauji took a pot shot at the producer. The set was ready and shooting was to commence when the rising star Amrish Puri arrived. It was decided that they would shoot with Amrish Puri first and thereafter proceed with the day's work, so everybody waited and waited. When the waiting became too long, Madanji said in a stage whisper, 'I had one remaining ambition in life and that was to work with Subhash Ghai. I fear that this wish will remain unfulfilled.' Subhash Ghai got the message and soon work resumed for all.

'The ship sequence in *Kranti* was shot over eighteen days. One day Madanji arrived with a young and very attractive film journalist. Towards the end of the day's work, Shatrughan Sinha asked the girl if she felt afraid amongst so many men. She innocently replied, "As long as I am with Maddi uncle, I have nothing to fear." That deflated our "Maddi uncle"; the rest of the cast ribbed him for days.'

# AMJAD KHAN

One of the most famous character roles in the history of Bollywood, was Amjad Khan as Gabbar Singh in *Sholay*. Sadly, due to his early death, Amjad could never ever reach the heights of fame and creativity, which Gabbar Singh had provided him with.

According to Tom Alter, Amjad Khan and Bauji had to finalise a wicked deal. Madanji's dialogue was '*Agar tum hamara yeh kaam kar doge to hum tumhe mun manga inaam denge.*' The shot was ready and the camera rolled. Madanji said, '*Agar tum hamare yeh kaam kardoge to hum tumhare mun men denge.*' I'm not going to translate this here for those who don't understand Hindi because it is rather risqué and best not elaborated on! Amjad collapsed in a fit of laughter, and it was only when order had been restored that the shooting could recommence. Amjad Khan also came to pay his last respects at his co-worker's funeral.

## RAJ KUMAR KOHLI

When I met Kohli Saab at his office in Santa Cruz, he said that it was very difficult to give me specific anecdotes about Madan Puri because he was a perfect gentleman in all his dealings.

Kohli Saab asked me the purpose of my research. I said I wanted to make a record so that future generations would know that there was a great and good man in our family. Kohli Saab said that I was very lucky, because my father's movies would live on for years and many generations would be able to see him. He was immortal. Producers and directors and other technicians would also live through their work, but future generations would not be able to see them as living and walking beings. Kohli Saab said that he had come across very few actors in this industry who could match his performance. He was an artist of rare calibre. Madan Puri worked with him for *Kahani Hum Sab Ki* (1973), Jaani Dushman (1974), *Muqabla* (1979), *Badle Ki Aag* (1982), *Naukar Biwi Ka* (1983), *Raj Tilak* (1984), *Saazish* (1988).

## PRAN SAHEB

In a discussion with *Star and Style* (30 March 1973) Madan Puri had said, 'Pran is one of my closest and oldest friends in the film industry. We knew each other since 1937 from Shimla when I was in government service and he was a photographer. Pran is most fantastically professional. When he takes up any assignment, you know that for a full two months before shooting starts the script writer, the assistant directors, the director, the make-up man, the wig maker and everybody else needed for his work – they will be drinking whisky at his house at Pran's expense and discussing the project. He goes into every detail about his role and for this reason I have been a great admirer of his. While he is a few years younger than me yet as an actor he is senior to me as he started working in Lahore much before me.' Today, he is amongst the most senior artistes in the industry and he ranks in fame and popularity amongst the best. His punctuality and sincerity is legendary. Once he has arrived, he will wait patiently for his call. He will not leave the set till it is pack up time. This interview was reproduced in… *and Pran – a biography* by Bunny Reuben in 2005.

Pran and Bauji worked together in twenty-nine movies: *Gambler* (1960), *Kashmir Ki Kali* (1964), *Shaheed* (1965), *Gumnaam* (1965), *Tumse Achha Kaun Hai* (1969), *Jaal Saaz* (1969), *Pyaar Hi Pyaar* (1969), *Yaadgaar* (1969), *Purab aur Paschim* (1970), *Bhai Bhai* (1970), *Laakhon Mein Ek* (1971), *Sazaa* (1972), *Gaddaar* (1973), *Dharma* (1973), *Joshila* (1973), *Majboor* (1974), *Zahreela Insaan* (1975), *Warrant* (1975), *Khalifa* (1976), *Chakkar pe Chakkar* (1977), *Vishwanath* (1978), *Zaalim* (1980), *Dhan Daulat* (1980), *Khuda Kasam* (1981), *Badle Ki Aag* (1982), *Who Jo Haseena* (1983), *Naastik* (1983), *Raja Tilak* (1984), *Yudh* (1985).

## JEETENDRA

I was the Secretary of the Willingdon Sports Club at Haji Ali and lived on the Club premises. In 2000, my wife and I returned to our residence after the Club's Holi festivities. Just then the watchman excitedly announced the arrival of Jeetendra, who was returning to Bandra after visiting his childhood home in Girgaum. His escort mentioned that Madan Puri's son lived in the Club, and on an impulse he drove in. 'I am sorry to have come in unannounced, but I miss Madanji very much and I came to pay my respects,' he said. He stayed only a few minutes, but he had stolen our hearts by showing so much respect and affection for my father.

## MADHAV AGASHE

Bauji was a thrifty man by nature and by upbringing. He understood the hardship a producer goes through in the making of a film, and always tried to reduce his financial burden. He never demanded a bigger make-up room, special meals, or anything not integral to the making of a film. However, he insisted on high quality dresses, wigs, beard; whatever his role demanded. He had no special tailor or wig maker, but whenever he came across a sincere, dedicated and competent worker he would recommend him. One such person was Madhav Agashe, a small time tailor. Bauji always used him and recommended him to Amrish chachaji. Soon, 'Mogambo' became a one-man industry and Madhav flourished. Today he is a famous name not only in the film industry but also in political and social circles.

Madhav told me that he always had a stock of suits ready for Madan Puri Saab. About five years after Bauji's demise, I had some clothes tailored from Madhav's *Men's Modes*. When I asked for the bill he refused to charge anything, which I could not accept. Finally he produced a small tin box from his cash box. With trembling hands he opened the box and produced a crumpled hundred-rupee note and a one-rupee coin. In a voice heavy with emotion he said, 'Many years ago Puri Saab backed me and I became Madhav's *Men's Modes* from Madho. He gave me this money as a good luck charm and I have grown with his blessings.' We both wept, remembering the goodness of Madan Puri. After much persuasion he accepted a token amount. When Bauji passed away, Madhav brought a shawl that he had personally prepared the previous night.

## AMIN SAYANI

Post–Independence, Radio Ceylon provided a never-ending supply of Hindi film music. Amin Sayani was a popular Hindustani and English broadcaster on Radio Ceylon. Those who grew up in the sixties and seventies will remember radio programs like *Binaca Geet Mala* and S Kumar's *Filmi Mulakat* and *Filmi Muqadama*. Radio Ceylon also broadcast the commercial services of All India Radio under the banner of Vividh Bharathi.

In July 2012, St Xavier's College was holding a seminar to celebrate one hundred years of the Indian Film Industry. Mr Amin Sayani, who was one of the listed speakers, spoke of his memories of Madan Puri. He later gave me a CD of two interviews with Madan Puri, taped for S Kumar Sarees and titled *Filmi Mulaqat* and *Filmi Mukadama*. They were recorded in the seventies and gave me some more insight into Bauji's work.

In *Filmi Muqadama*, Bauji said that it was his childhood desire to act in movies. His first experience was working in Lahore in *Khazanchi* (1941) where a song sequence *Sawan ke Nazaare*, was shot in the Botanical Gardens. Shaukat Hussein Rizvi was the song director and Mahendra Malhotra was the cameraman. Mr Malhotra told Bauji that he had talent and a photogenic face and he must persevere with his work in movies.

Some extracts from his interview are: 'The going was very tough initially but if there is no Autumn then where is the pleasure in Spring... Nobody praises the villains. We take the beatings while the heroes get the applause... Every parent loves to see his child as a hero; my father came to see one of my movies and when he saw

In *Aatish (1979)*

In *Geeta Gata Chal (1975)*

In *Rafoo Chakkar (1975)*

With Shakti Samanta, Chaman Puri, Sapru and Randhir at the premier of *Goonj* (1952)

With Surendra

With S D Burman

With his wife

On his first grandchild's birthday (1970)

With his brothers Amrish & Chaman (*above*)
Madan Puri's Sons - Peshi, Bobli and Kamli (*below*)

With Iftekhar in *Dulhan Wohi Jo Piya Man Bhaye* (1977)

In *Geet Gata Chal* ( 1975)

Surprise birthday party on sets with Amrish Puri, Pran, Dev Anand and others

Receiving an award from the Federation of UP Film Journalists

With Shashi Kapoor at the premiere of *Chor Machaye Shor* (1974) in Ratlam

With Hemant Kumar, Biswajit and others

स नरसित याद आ जाती हैं जिन्होंने
हृदय महारानी की तरह स्टूडियो में
ासन किया. और ऐसा शासन किया
ह सभी जनका गुणगान करने लगे थे.
और: आज, मत पूछो, किसके दिल
। क्या गुजर रही है.

### दनपुरी को हीरो बनना
अच्छा नहीं लगा

| यदि आज किसी खलनायक को
रो बना दीजिए तो यह समझेगा,
सका भाग्य खुल गया है. पर एक
मय ऐसा था जब मदनपुरी को हीरो
नाया गया तो उन्हें यह अच्छा नहीं
गा. बात यह भी कि जीवन संघर्ष
रने के बाद और जीवन का गहरा
नुभव करने के बाद फिल्मों में आये

ये. उन दिनों उनमें जोश-खरोश था.
पर जब वे फिल्मों में हीरो बने तो
उन्हें अनुभव हुआ कि वे जिंदगी से
बहुत दूर हैं. यह क्या कि हीरो-हीरो-
इन के पीछे नाच रहा है, कूद रहा है
और गाना गा रहा है. हीरो के रोल
उन्हें इतने ठंडे लगे, इतने ठंडे लगे
कि मन बार-बार हीरो से अलग जोश
वाली भूमिकाएँ करने को मचल पड़ा.

संयोग की बात यह हुई कि जिन
बार-पांच फिल्मों के वे हीरो बने, वह
बॉक्स-ऑफिस पर फेल हो गयीं.
दर्शकों ने भी उन्हें हीरो के रूप में
स्वीकार नहीं किया. यदि मदनपुरी
की जगह और कोई होता तो
उसे बनती फिल्मों के फ्लाप होने पर
गहरा आघात लगता. पर मदनपुरी

ने समझा, चलो हीरो न सही, खल-
नायक ही सही. वे खलनायक बनने
की तोड़-फूड करने लगे और भाग्य से
उन्हें देव आनंद और सुरैया के साथ
खलनायक की बोंबसी और प्रभा-
कारी भूमिका करने का अवसर मिल
गया. वह यही चाहते थे. यह भी
संयोग की बात कि खलनायक बनते ही
ही भारतों और उनकी जिंदगी का धारा
जोश-खरोश खलनायकों की भूमिकाओं
में उमड़ पड़ा और मन की इच्छा-
नुसार ऊँचे दर्जे के खलनायक बन
थवे.

# Filmfans Federation of India

This Certificate of HONOUR is granted to

*Madan Puri*

Who has been adjudged a winner of

**FILMFANS
AWARD-73.**
(MOST RATIONAL & GENUINE AWARD)

for bringing happiness in the life of millions of Filmfans worldover through his / her contribution as

*"Best Character Actor"
Anurag*

In testimony whereof a trophy of the Federation has been presented by Hon. Dr. M. B. POPAT, Minister for Prohibition of Maharastra, today the Nineteenth day of April 1974.

(Dr. S. M. SINGH SUMAN)
(Vice Chancellor, Vikram University)
Vice Chairman, Panel of Judges

[PRAKASH VEER SHASTRI M. P.]
Chairman,
Panel of Judges

(N. D. SNATAK Ex. M. P.)
[Chairman, Rly. Service Commission ]
President.

(RAVI SHARMA)
F. I. L. E. A. M. I. St. E., M. I. S. E
Member Secretary to Panel of Judges

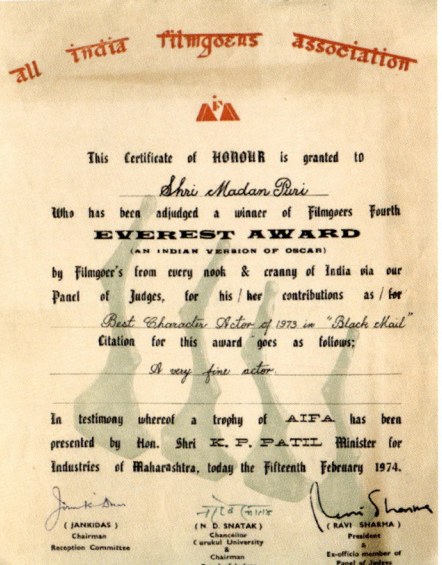

# all india filmgoers association

This Certificate of HONOUR is granted to

*Shri Madan Puri*

Who has been adjudged a winner of Filmgoers Fourth

**EVEREST AWARD**
(AN INDIAN VERSION OF OSCAR)

by Filmgoer's from every nook & cranny of India via our Panel of Judges, for his / her contributions as / for

*Best Character Actor of 1973 in "Black Mail"*

Citation for this award goes as follows;

*A very fine actor.*

In testimony whereof a trophy of AIFA has been presented by Hon. Shri K. P. PATIL Minister for Industries of Maharashtra, today the Fifteenth February 1974.

( JANKIDAS )
Chairman
Reception Committee

( N. D. SNATAK )
Chancellor
Gurukul University
&
Chairman
Panel of Judges

( RAVI SHARMA )
President
&
Ex-official member of
Panel of Judges

Signing autogrpahs for fans

In *Sautela Pati* (1986)

me doing a negative role and being abused by the audience, he left the movie hall.'

I am grateful to Mr Amin Sayani for his valuable inputs.

## 'LAUGHTER CLUB' – OM PRAKASH / PRAN / MADAN PURI

Pran, Om Prakash and Madan Puri started a laughter club during the shoots. They felt that everybody took themselves and their work very seriously. They would sit together and tell jokes and laugh. If anybody wanted to join in they first had to tell a good joke.

Once the three great artistes went to Jodhpur for shooting. After the day's pack-up, they sat in one of the rooms gossiping and drinking. They informed the hotel staff that they would be going to town for dinner. By the time they moved out the town had closed down. The three spent the night very hungry and unhappy.

Rajendranath's favourite quote in the presence of Madan Puri was, 'I am very fond of my junior colleagues like Chintu Baba, Chimpu Baba and Madan Baba.'

Dinesh Raheja and Jitendra Kothari in their book, *Indian Cinema: THE BOLLYWOOD SAGA*, had this to say about Madan Puri, '*Prem Pujari* proved that age had not dulled this old reprobate's saw-toothed flair for chicanery.'

Some of the stars that Madan Puri worked with are (in alphabetical order): Amitabh Bachhan (11 movies), Asha Parekh (12), Dev Anand (14), Dharmendra (18), Hema Malini (14), Jeetendra (13), Kamini Kaushal (11), Manoj Kumar (15), Manmohan Krishna (18), Neetu Singh (9), Pran (29), Prem Chopra (38), Rajesh Khanna (22), Rajinder Kumar (10), Randhir Kapoor (8) Ranjeet (14), Rishi Kapoor (7) Rekha (11), Reena Roy (16), Saira Banu (11), Shatrughan Sinha (19), Sharmila Tagore (12), Shashi Kapoor (24).

# 18 | THE FINAL DAYS

On 8 May 1984 our parents attended a marriage in Delhi at which Bauji was, as usual, the centre of attention and full of life. The day after the reception, they were to take a train to Kota to celebrate my birthday the next day. Bauji loved travelling by train. He enjoyed interacting with the public and often observed those he met as characters that he could play in his movies. His powers of observation were acute.

At some point late in the night he woke up Beeji and said, 'I want to go to Bombay. I am in a hurry, so let us go by air… Ring up Kamli, and ask them to come to Bombay to celebrate his birthday.'

His urgency was inexplicable. The next morning they flew to Bombay. From then on his health deteriorated. We always wonder what premonition he had on the night of 8 May 1984 that made him rush back to Bombay. For the next eight months he moved from hospital to hospital and underwent multiple tests and treatment for cancer.

By the end of 1984, Bauji was wasting away. Harish chachaji's daughter was getting married in Pune and the date was fixed for 16 January 1985. Bauji, aware that he might not be around on the wedding date, made a special trip to Pune to bless her. Too weak to walk, he had to be carried up and down the stairs.

He had given clear instructions that the marriage would not be postponed for any reason, and my mother insisted that we three brothers must attend the marriage ceremony, which we did the night after Bauji's funeral. His ashes were not yet cold.

All his friends and colleagues came to see him in the hospital, and everybody pretended that he would soon be well. For some, it was like a pilgrimage. There were people whom we had never seen or heard of before – people whom Bauji had befriended when their luck was down. We met the hospital lift operators with whom Bauji had shared a pleasant moment. The nurses and the ward boys and the junior doctors dropped in. Jokingly, Bauji would always say, 'Are you going to charge me consultancy fees for this visit or do I charge you for the interview?' Some of the senior doctors would come in, say a few words and go away, wet-eyed. The early days of January 1985 were the most poignant.

In the final days, the doctors at Breach Candy put him on dialysis. While in a semi-conscious state, he kept mumbling to himself; some of the words were *Kyamari* and *Clifton*. I asked Beeji what it meant, and she said that he was remembering the names of the local railway stations of Karachi where he had served in 1938–39; perhaps reliving his past one last time.

Breach Candy allowed only one person to stay overnight. Beeji refused to move out of the hospital for even a moment. I had spent very little time with him in the last year, so at night I would wait in the toilet when the nurse-on-duty came to check for visitors. They knew I was there, but the charade had to be played out.

A couple of days before his demise he sent for his grandchildren, Kanchan, Sonal and Vikram. He hugged each one, shedding tears of regret for the growing-up years and the weddings that he would miss, the great-grandchildren he would never see.

Bauji was a faint heartbeat away from immortality and his once strong voice was fading away to join the primordial OM. At about four pm the doctors told us that the end was imminent. The family assembled at his bedside: his wife and sons and their families, Chaman Puri and Harish Puri, and their families were also present. Amrish Puri had flown to Bangalore that morning to complete an urgent shooting of *Meri Jung,* but his wife and children were present. Chandrakanta and her husband, Rajesh Mehra, had come in from Delhi. She was reciting the *Gayatri Mantra* and making Bauji repeat it, and the family recited the mantra with him. He had always recited *Hanuman Chalisa* while having his bath, and *Gayatri Mantra* while travelling back and forth to work, or in moments of stress. His voice became a whisper; our recital became more fervent. The whisper faded away. The end came at 6.15 pm on 13 January 1985.

Bauji was moved to the Breach Candy Hospital morgue, and we returned to a silent home. No more would we hear the familiar sound of Bauji's footsteps climbing the stairs. Every night the house used to come alive when he entered: now the laughter was gone from our lives, and we were left only with memories. We ate dinner sent in by the neighbours; what amazed me was that we could eat at all. Our dog Danny knew that his master had gone away; he went under the sofa and refused to come out.

Amrish chachaji returned the same night, grieved to know that Bauji had already left the world. Now friends and relatives had to be informed and arrangements made for the funeral. Phone calls kept pouring in throughout the night. The newspapers and TV constantly carried items about him and his life.

The next morning we went to Breach Candy to bring him back home for a last few moments on his favourite carpet. Despite our sorrow, we had a light moment when we learnt that Bauji had spent his last night on earth next to an unknown lady in the morgue!

# EPILOGUE

In the shadow of death, life must go on. On January 16, barely two days after Bauji's funeral, we three brothers attended the wedding of Harish chachaji's daughter at Beeji's insistence.

Whenever Bauji visited us in Ambala or Chandigarh, a trip to Haridwar was a must. The dip in the cold rushing waters of the Ganges has a special charm. Peshi, Ramnesh and I immersed our father's ashes at Har-ki-Pauri, and watched the red cloth covering them float away. Yet Bauji had never seemed closer. We then went on to Kurukshetra to perform some pujas, and returned to Bombay.

By the end of January all the mourners had departed and the priests had been fed and given gifts, again and again. There were some legal formalities to be handled as per Beeji's directions. It was time for us to get back to work and a normal life, and Bauji would have liked it that way.

About a year earlier Peshi had rented a place in Parsi Colony, near Punjabi Galli, but had not moved there due to Bauji's illness. A couple of months after the funeral he and Veena moved house, but continued to spend the day at Punjabi Galli, while Vikram went back to school. Vikram is now married to Madhuli Mittal. Ramnesh resumed work, and Gayatri was at home.

The Army sent me from Kota to Trichy for two years and then to Srinagar for the next two years. In 1986 Kanchan moved to Bombay to study at the JJ School of Architecture.

In 1989, I was posted to Montreal on an Indo-Canada Youth Exchange Program as a coordinator. I moved my family to Bombay, into the AFI Building next to Metro Cinema. On my return from Canada I took two years' study leave to pursue a Ph.D. in Indo-US Relations. Kanchan finished her studies, and a couple of years later Sonal also joined the Architecture course.

In 1991, Kanchan married her college friend Kiran Shetty, who had studied architecture with her. We held a grand wedding, which would have gladdened Bauji's heart.

Sonal finished her B Arch. in 1995 and took admission at University of Southern California, Los Angeles, for her Master's in Architecture. Kanchan had attended the same two-year program after her marriage.

In 1995 I completed my Ph.D. In the same year Sonal met Gaurav Singh at USC, where he was pursuing a Master's in Electrical Engineering. They married in California in July 2000 and had a traditional wedding in India six months later.

On 27 December 2003, my mother passed away. Ramnesh's wife Gayatri had also passed away some months earlier, leaving two lovely children. Amrit, now married to Neha Mishra, works with the Times Group as Senior Accounts Manager for Movies Now and Romedy Now. Ishita is a writer and associate director making TV serials.

In 2002, while visiting Sonal in Santa Clara, California, Renuka had fallen ill. She was in and out of hospitals in Bombay for the next three years, and passed away on 24 February 2005. Renuka was the anchor of our existence and her death left us shattered.

Amrish chachaji had died six weeks earlier on 12 January 2005.

In July 2006 I met Jane Bhandari, a writer and designer who had come to India in 1967 after marrying Arun Bhandari, an engineer. He died in 1997.

Jane and I were married on 23 December 2012. Jane's son and daughter joined forces with my two girls to arrange the perfect Indian wedding, and did us proud. Madhu and her husband Ehsaan Noorani, Tarun and his partner Shonali, Kanchan and Sonal and their husbands Kiran and Gaurav and my four grandchildren Kunal, Kehan, Rayan and Reyna, did everything possible to make it a joyful and memorable event.

Kanchan's friends, Ravi and Kalpana, provided the venue for the sangeet. Anjali and Ishan Raina threw open their home to provide the perfect setting for the wedding. My old friend Pesi Wadia gave us his huge garden for the reception. Suneeta Rao, Shankar Mahadevan, Ehsaan, and Sivamani kept the guests enthralled by their music.

My cousin Dalip Laroiya graduated from IIT, Bombay. He married Jyotsna Naik, an air-hostess with British Airways. They have hosted us many times in their Delhi home.

I take my IPod with me on my morning walk, and listen to Hanuman Chalisa and Gayatri Mantra, and then some film music. In Amar Prem, Bauji as Nepali Babu meets Rajesh Khanna in Calcutta's red light area, and says, *Arre Anand Babu aap aur yahan!! Aapne pehchane nahin mujhe – aayie, aiye na.*

I hear my father's voice in that scene just before the song, and for a few quiet moments he comes alive again for me.

# MOVIE LINE UP

*Santosh* (1989)
DIRECTOR: Balbir Wadhawan
CAST: Manoj Kumar, Hema Malini, Prem Chopra, Rakhi, Abhi Bhattacharya, Kamini Kaushal, Nirupa Roy, Sarika, Shatrughan Sinha

*Saazish* (1988)
DIRECTOR: Raj Kumar Kohli
CAST: Raaj Kumar, Mithun, Raaj Babbar, Dimple, Vinod Mehra, Anita Raaj, Shakti Kapoor
CHARACTER: Kaka

*Madadgar* (1987)
DIRECTOR: Ramnesh Puri
CAST: Jeetendra, Sulakshana Pandit, Amrish Puri, Ranjeet, Aruna Irani, Om Shivpuri, Lalita Pawar

*Vishaal* (1987)
DIRECTOR: Dinesh
CAST: Vinod Mehra, Bindiya Goswami, Kulbhushan Kharbanda
CHARACTER: Laawaris

*Ghulami ki Zanjeerein* (1987)

*Khel Mohabbat Ka* (1986)
DIRECTOR: Satish Duggal
CAST: Faroukh Shaikh, Poonam Dhillon, Shakti Kapoor, Prema Narayan
CHARACTER: Rehman

*Sautela Pati* (1986)
DIRECTOR: B R Ishara
CAST: Raj Kiran, Asha Sachdev, Navin Nischol, Gulshan Grover
CHARACTER: Madan

*Cheekh* (1985)
DIRECTOR: P Mohan Bhakri

CAST: Javed Khan, Amala, Neelam Mehra, Rajendra Nath

*Baadal* (1985)
DIRECTOR: Anand Sagar
CAST: Shammi Kapoor, Mithun, Poonam Dhillon, Arun Govil, Shakti Kapoor
CHARACTER: Thakur

*Babu* (1985)
DIRECTOR: A R Trilogchandra
CAST: Rajesh Khanna, Hema Malini, Navin Nischol, Deepak Parasher, Rati Agnihotri, Mala Sinha, Agha, Om Shivpuri, Rajendra Nath, Paintal, Mukri
CHARACTER: MLA Shambhu Nath

*Jhoothi* (1985)
DIRECTOR: Hrishikesh Mukherjee
CAST: Rekha, Raj Babbar, Amol Palekar
CHARACTER: Professor Puri

*Bepanaah* (1985)
DIRECTOR: Jagdish Sidhana
CAST: Shashi Kapoor, Mithun, Poonam Dhillon, Rati Aghnihotri, Suresh Oberoi

*Yudh* (1985)
DIRECTOR: Rajiv Rai
CAST: Jackie Shroff, Tina Munim, Anil Kapoor, Nutan, Hema Malini, Pran, Manmohan Krishna, Shatrughan Sinha
CHARACTER: Dayal

*Jawaab* (1985)
DIRECTOR: Ravi Tandon
CAST: Raj Babbar, Smita Patil, Abhi Bhattacharya, Danny, Parikshit Sahni
CHARACTER: Lakhani

*Lavaa* (1985)
DIRECTOR: Rajindra Peepat
CAST: Raj Babbar, Dimple Kapadia, Asha Parekh, Rajiv Kapoor

*Maujaan Dubai Diyaan* (1985)
DIRECTOR: Subhash Bhakri
CAST: Mithun, Bhavana Bhatt, Aruna Irani, Vinod Mehra, Ranjeet, Raza Murad

*Ulta Seedha* (1985)
DIRECTOR: Subodh Mukherjee
CAST: Raj Babbar, Rati Agnihotri, Utpal Dutt, Aruna Irani, Deven Verma, Agha
CHARACTER: Colonel

*Yaadon Ki Kasam* (1985)
DIRECTOR: Vinod Dewan
CAST: Mithun, Zeenat Aman, Asrani
CHARACTER: Kapoor

*Damaad Chaiye* (1985)
DIRECTOR: CAST: Benjamin Gilani, Priyadarshani

# MADAN PURI PASSED AWAY ON 13 JANUARY 1985

*Lorie* (1984)
DIRECTOR: Vijay Talwar
CAST: Faroukh Sheikh, Naseerudin Shah, Shabana Azmi, Paresh Rawal
CHARACTER: Mr Kapoor

*Baazi* (1984)
DIRECTOR: Raj N Sippy
CAST: Dharmendra, Mithun, Rekha, Ranjeeta, Shakti Kapoor, Prema Nararyan

*Asha Jyoti* (1984)
DIRECTOR: Narayan Rao Dasari
CAST: Rajesh Khanna, Rekha, Reena Roy, Shakti Kapoor
CHARACTER: Seth Badri Prasad

*Mashaal* (1984)
DIRECTOR: Yash Chopra
CAST: Dilip Kumar, Anil Kapoor, Amrish Puri, Rati Agnihotri, Waheeda Rehman
CHARACTER: Tolaram

*Aaj Ka M.L.A. Ram Avtar....* (1984)
DIRECTOR: Narayan Rao Dasari

CAST: Rajesh Khanna, Shabana Azmi, Shatrughan Sinha, Jagdeep, Deven Verma, A K Hangal
CHARACTER: Makhanlal Kesri

*Awaaz* (1984)
DIRECTOR: Shakti Samantha
CAST: Rajesh Khanna, Jaya Pradha, Prem Chopra, Amrish Puri, Rakesh Roshan, Iftekhar
CHARACTER: Mirchandan

*Khazana* (1984)
DIRECTOR: Harmesh Malhotra
CAST: Randhir Kapoor, Rekha, Bindu, Dev Kumar

*Raaj Tilak* (1984)
DIRECTOR: Raj Kumar Kohli
CAST: Dharmendra, Hema Malini, Pran, Raj Kumar, Reena Roy, Ajit, Ranjeeta, Ranjit, Sarika, Yogeeta Bali, Kamal Hassan
CHARACTER: Ranjeet

*Waqt Ki Pukar* (1984)
DIRECTOR: Desh Gautam
CAST: Vijayendra Ghatghe, Ranjit, Yogeeta Bali, Raj Kiran
CHARACTER: Subedhar

*Yaadon Ki Zanjeer* (1984)
DIRECTOR: Shibhu Mitra
CAST: Sunil Dutt, Shashi Kapoor, Reena Roy, Shabana Azami, Kader Khan, Agha

*Raja Aur Rana* (1984)
DIRECTOR: Shibhu Mitra
CAST: Ashok Kumar, Pran, Ajit, Chandrashekar, Punit Issar, Om Prakash

*Sardar* (1984)
DIRECTOR: N Harish Chandra Rao
CAST: Mohan Babu, Jaya Prada, Sharda

*Tarkeeb* (1984)
DIRECTOR: Ravikant Nagaich
CAST: Mithun, Ranjeeta, Shakti, Paintal

*Tere Mere Beech Mein* (1984)
DIRECTOR: Dada Kondke
CAST: Amjad Khan, Dada Kondke, Usha Chavan, Jayshree T

*Agar Tum Na Hote* (1983)
DIRECTOR: Lekh Tandon
CAST: Rajesh Khanna, Rekha, Raj Babbar, Asrani, Sunder
CHARACTER: Shakur

*Sweekar Kiya Maine* (1983)
DIRECTOR: Zaheer D Lairi
CAST: Vinod Mehra, Shabana Azmi, Prema Narayan

*Nastik* (1983)
DIRECTOR: Pramod Chakravorty
CAST: Amitabh Bachhan, Hema Malini, Pran, Amjad Khan, Bharat Bhooshan, Kamal Kapoor, Bhagwan, Nalini Jaywant, Shammi, Lalita Pawar
CHARACTER: P I Ganga Ram

*Andha Kanoon* (1983)
DIRECTOR: Rama Rao Tatineni
CAST: Amitabh Bachhan, Hema Malini, Rajnikant, Reena Roy, Pran, Prem Chopra, Danny, Amrish Puri and Dharmendra
CHARACTER: Jailor Gupta

*Avtaar* (1983)
DIRECTOR: Mohan Kumar
CAST: Rajesh Khanna, Shabana Azmi, Sachin
CHARACTER: Jugal Kishor

*Dharti Aakash* (TV) (1983)
DIRECTOR: Ram Gabale
CAST: Iftekar, Prem Kishen, Kaajal Kiran
CHARACTER: Jagdish

*Hero* (1983)
DIRECTOR: Subhas Ghai
CAST: Sanjeev Kumar, Meenakshi Sheshadri, Shammi Kapoor, Jackie Shroff
CHARACTER: Bharat

*Humse Na Jeeta Koi* (1983)
DIRECTOR: Shibhu Mitra
CAST: Randhir Kapoor, Shoma Anand, Amjad Khan, Jeevan, Shakti Kapoor, Ranjeeta
CHARACTER: Girdhari

*Main Awara Hoon* (1983)
DIRECTOR: Ashim Samanta
CAST: Sanjay Dutt, Raj Babbar, Jaya Pradha, Rati Agnihotri, Shoma Anand, Iftekhar

*Mazdoor* (1983)
DIRECTOR: Ravi Chopra
CAST: Dilip Kumar, Nanda, Raj Babbar, Rati Agnihotri, Padmini Kolhapure, Raj Kiran, Suresh Oberoi, Nasir Hussein, Iftekhar, Johnny Walker
CHARACTER: Daulatram

*Naukar Biwi Ka* (1983)
DIRECTOR: Raj Kumar Kohli

CAST: Dharmendra, Anita Raaj, Reena Roy, Raj Babbar, Kader Khan, Om Prakash, Rishi Kapoor
CHARACTER: Director

*Painter Babu* (1983)
DIRECTOR: Ashok
CAST: Rajiv Goswami, Meenakshi Sheshadri, Aruna Irani, Bharat Kapoor, Kamini Kaushal
CHARACTER: Mali Kaka

*Woh Jo Hasina* (1983)
DIRECTOR: Deepak Bahri
CAST: Mithun, Ranjeeta, Pran, Rajinder Nath, Kader Khan

*Mehendi* (1983)
DIRECTOR: Asit Sen
CAST: Raj Babbar, Vinod Mehra, Ranjeeta, Bindiya, Shakti Kapoor

*Paanchwin Manzil* (1983)
DIRECTOR: Jagdish Sidhana
CAST: Raj Babbar, Zarina Wahab, Shoma Anand

*Pyaas* (1983)
DIRECTOR: O P Ralhan
CAST: O P Ralhan, Zeenat Aman, Anju Mahendru, Tanuja

*Baade Dilwale* (1983)
DIRECTOR: Bhappie Sonie
CAST: Rishi Kapoor, Jyoti Bakshi, Roopesh Kumar

*Pyaar Bina Jag Soona* (1983)
DIRECTOR: Surinder Sinha
CAST: Arun Govil, Swaroop Sampath, Shoma Anand, Kalpana Aiyar, Rakesh Pandey

*Dard Ka Rishta* (1982)
DIRECTOR: Sunil Dutt
CAST: Ashok Kumar, Sunil Dutt, Padmini Kolhapuri, Reena Roy, Smita Patil

*Ayaash* (1982)
DIRECTOR: Shakti Samantha
CAST: Sanjiv Kumar, Agnihotri, Arun Govil, Helen, Chandrashekar
CHARACTER: Sansar

*Haathkadi* (1982)
DIRECTOR: Surendra Mohan
CAST: Sanjeev Kumar, Reena Roy, Shatrughan Sinha, Rakesh Roshan, Ranjeeta, Prem Chopra, Jeevan, Kanhaiyalal, Raj Mehra
CHARACTER: Harimohan's boss

*Apradhi Kaun?* (1982)
DIRECTOR: Mohan Bhakri
CAST: Rajani Sharma, Raza Murad, Iftekhar, Om Shivpuri
CHARACTER: Rai Bahadur

*Badle Ki Aag* (1982)
DIRECTOR: Raj Kumar Kohli
CAST: Sunil Dutt, Dharmendra, Jeetendra, Shatrughan Sinha, Reena Roy, Smita Patil, Sarika
CHARACTER: Mohanlal

*Dulha Bikta Hai* (1982)
DIRECTOR: Anwar Pasha
CAST: Raj Babbar, Anita Raj, Simple Kapadia
CHARACTER: Dad

*Ghazab* (1982)
DIRECTOR: C P Dixit
CAST: Dharmendra, Rekha, Ranjeet, Aruna Irani, Jagdeep
CHARACTER: Shankar

*Pyaas* (1982)
DIRECTOR: O P Ralhan
CAST: O P Ralhan, Zeenat Aman, Tanuja, Anju Mahendru

*Sawaal* (1982)
DIRECTOR: Ramesh Talwar
CAST: Shashi Kapoor, Sanjeev Kumar, Waheeda Rehman, Poonam Dhillon, Randhir Kapoor, Prem Chopra
CHARACTER: Govindram

*Vidhaata* (1982)
DIRECTOR: Subhash Ghai
CAST: Dilip Kumar, Shammi Kapoor, Sanjiv Kumar, Amrish Puri, Suresh Oberoi, Tom Alter
CHARACTER: K K

*Aadat Se Majboor* (1982)
DIRECTOR: Ambrish Sangal
CAST: Mithun, Ranjeeta, Amrish Puri, Rameshwari, Om Shivpuri

*Heeron Ka Chor* (1982)
DIRECTOR: S K Kapur
CAST: Mithun, Bindiya, Ashok Kumar

*Honey* (1982)
DIRECTOR: Sheetal
CAST: Bhagwan, Sheetal, Pradip Kumar, Asit Sen, Jagdeep

*Dil Mera Dharkan Teri* (1982)
DIRECTOR: Vijay Srivastav
CAST: Balraj, Nisha, Vijai Khote, Sonia Sahni, Jeevan

*Nai Imarat* (1981)
DIRECTOR: Ram Pahwa
CAST: Rakesh Pandey, Parikshit Sawhney, Ranjeeta, Sarika, Vidya Sinha, Sajjan, Amrish Puri, Asit Sen, Mohan Chotti, Chandrashekhar

*Sahhas* (1981)
DIRECTOR: Ravikant Nagaich
CAST: Mithun, Rati Agnihotri, Shakti Kapoor, Jagdeep
CHARACTER: Jaggan

*Khuda Kasam* (1981)
DIRECTOR: Lekh Tandon
CAST: Vinod Khanna, Tina Munim, Ajit, Pran, Kamini Kaushal, Shakti Kapoor
CHARACTER: Kishanlal

*Prem Geet* (1981)
DIRECTOR: Sudesh Issar
CAST: Raaj Babbar, Anita Raaj, Saajan, Rajni Sharma
CHARACTER: Bhardwaj

*Dahshat....* (1981)
DIRECTOR: Ramsay Brothers
CAST: Navin Nischol, Sarika, Nadira, Om Shivpuri
CHARACTER: Father

*Itni Si Baat* (1981)
DIRECTOR: Madhu M
CAST: Sanjiv Kumar, Moushami Chatterjee, Arun Govil
CHARACTER: Darbarilal

*Mangalsutra* (1981)
DIRECTOR: Vijay M
CAST: Rekha, Anant Nag, Prema Narayan, Om Shivpuri

*Kranti* (1981)
DIRECTOR: Manoj Kumar
CAST: Manoj Kumar, Dilip Kumar, Shashi Kapoor, Shatrughan Sinha, Hema Malini, Tom Alter
CHARACTER: Sher Singh

*Nakhuda* (1981)
DIRECTOR: Dilip Naik

CAST: Raj Kiran, Swaroop Sampat, Khulbhushan Kharbanda
CHARACTER: Jagannath

*Poonam* (1981)
DIRECTOR: Harmesh Malhotra
CAST: Raj Babbar, Poonam Dhillon, Jeevan, Shakti Kapoor

*Pyaasa Sawan* (1981)
DIRECTOR: Narayan Rao Dasari
CAST: Jeetendra, Reena Roy, Vinod Mehra, Moushumi Chatterjee, Aruna Irani
CHARACTER: Prabhudas

*Sharada* (1981)
DIRECTOR: Lekh Tandon
CAST: Raj Babbar, Jeetendra, Sarika, Kalpana Iyer
CHARACTER: Mr Kohli

*Josh* (1981)
DIRECTOR: Raj N Sippy
CAST: Amjad Khan, Raj Kiran, Sarika, Deven Verma, Vidya Sinha, Helen, Shakti Kapoor

*Chuppa Chuppi* (1981)
DIRECTOR: Arun Jaitley
CAST: Deven Verma, Aruna Irani, Shammi, Sunder, Paintal, Keshto, Bhagwan, Tun Tun, Helen, Seema Deo, Master Vikas, Bharat Dave, Inder Kumar, Satyan Kappu

*Nari* (1981)
DIRECTOR: Sham A Chand
CAST: Rakesh Roshan, Sarika

*Aap To Aise Na The* (1980)
DIRECTOR: Ambrish Sangal
CAST: Raj Babbar, Ranjeeta, Deepak Prasher, Raj Mehra
CHARACTER: Khanna

*Dhan Daulat* (1980)
DIRECTOR: Harish Rao
CAST: Rajinder Kumar, Mala Sinha, Rishi Kapoor, Neetu Singh, Pran, Premnath, Prem Chopra
CHARACTER: Father

*Humkadam* (1980)
DIRECTOR: Anil Ganguli
CAST: Biswajeet, Rakhee, Parikshit Sahni, Iftekhar
CHARACTER: Hariprasad

*Alibaba Aur 40 Chor* (1980)
DIRECTOR: Umesh Mehra

CAST: Dharmendra, Hema Malini, Zeenat Aman, Prem Chopra
CHARACTER: Dad

*Abdullah* (1980)
DIRECTOR: Sanjay Khan
CAST: Raj Kapoor, Sanjay Khan, Zeenat Aman, Sanjeev Kumar, Parveen Babi, Danny Denzongpa
CHARACTER: Commander

*Bandish* (1980/I)
DIRECTOR: K Bapaiah
CAST: Rajesh Khanna, Hema Malini, Danny, Tanuja, Om Prakash, Jeevan, Nalini Jaywant

*Desh Drohi* (1980)
DIRECTOR: Prakash Mehra
CAST: Saira Banu

*Hum Nahin Sudherenge* (1980)
DIRECTOR: Asrani
CAST: Asrani, Bharat Kapoor, Rita Bhaduri, Tom Alter, Sunder

*Khwab* (1980)
DIRECTOR: Shakti Samantha
CAST: Mithun, Ranjeeta, Ashok Kumar, Yogeeta Bali

*Lahoo Pukarega* (1980)
DIRECTOR: Akhtar – ul - Iman
CAST: Sunil Dutt, Manmohan Krishna

*Saajan Mere Main Saajan Ki* (1980)
DIRECTOR: Hiren Nag
CAST: Raj Kiran, Kajaal Kiron, Rameshwari, Ashok Kumar, Shashikala

*Shaitan Mujrim* (1980)
DIRECTOR: Nazar Khan
CAST: Rajesh Khanna, Raza Murad, Rakesh Roshan

*Taxi Chor* (1980)
DIRECTOR: Sushil Vyas
CAST: Mithun, Zarina Wahab

*Zalim* (1980)
DIRECTOR: Subhash Babbar
CAST: Vinod Khanna, Leena Chandervarkar, Pran, Iftekhar

*The Burning Train* (1980)
DIRECTOR: Ravi Chopra
CAST: Dharmendra, Hema Malini, Vinod Khanna, Parveen Babi, Jeetendra, Neetu Singh, Danny, Vinod Mehra, Navin Nischol, Asrani, Ranjeet
CHARACTER: Ashok's Dad

*Gadaar (1980)*
DIRECTOR: Harmesh Malhotra
CAST: Vinod Khanna, Yogeeta Bali

*Ek Baar Kaho* (1980)
DIRECTOR: Lekh Tandon
CAST: Anil Kapoor, Shabana Azmi, Navin Nischol,
Suresh Oberoi
Dr Puri

*Ek Gunah Aur Sahi* (1980)
DIRECTOR: Yogi Kathuria
CAST: Sunil Dutt, Parveen Babi
CHARACTER: Dubey

*Judaai* (1980)
DIRECTOR: Rama Rao Tatieni
CAST: Ashok Kumar, Jeetendra, Rekha

*Patita* (1980)
DIRECTOR: L V Sasi
CAST: Mithun, Shoma Anand, Raj Kiran

*Swayamvar* (1980)
DIRECTOR: V Sambasivam Rao
CAST: Shashi Kapoor, Sanjeev Kumar, Moushumi
Chatterjee, Vidya Sinha
CHARACTER: Makhanlal

*Yeh Kaisa Insaaf* (1980)
DIRECTOR: Narayan Rao Dasari
CAST: Vinod Mehra, Shabana Azmi, Sarika, Raj
Kiran

*Kismat Ki Baazi* (1980)
DIRECTOR: Bhappie Soni
CAST: Sharmila Tagore, Mithun Chakraborty,
Reena Roy, Prem Chopra, Jagdeep, Madan Puri

*Aakhri Kasam* (1979)
DIRECTOR: Ramnesh Puri
CAST: Vinod Mehra, Yogeeta Bali, Kabir Bedi

*Aatish* (1979)
DIRECTOR: Ambrish Sangal
CAST: Jeetendra, Neetu Singh, Dheeraj Kumar

*Badmashon Ka Badmash* (1979)
DIRECTOR: Satish Bhakhri
CAST: Satish Kaul, Bhavna Bhatt

*Lok Parlok* (1979)
DIRECTOR: Rama Rao Tatiani
CAST: Jeetendra, Jayapradha, Prem Nath

*Muqabla* (1979)
DIRECTOR: Raj Kumar Kohli

CAST: Rajesh Khanna, Sunil Dutt, Premnath, Ranjit,
Manmohan Krishna, Shatrughan Sinha, Rekha,
Reena Roy, Bindya Goswami, Ranjeet

*Raakhi Ki Saugandh* (1979)
DIRECTOR: Shibhu Mitra
CAST: Vinod Mehra, Sarika, Amjad Khan

*Shabash Daddy* (1979)
DIRECTOR: Kishore Kumar
CAST: Kishore Kumar, Amit Kumar, Yogeeta Bali

*Tere Pyare Mein* (1979)
DIRECTOR: Subash Sharma
CAST: Mithun Chakravorty, Sarika, Vijendra
Ghatge, Nadira, Iftekhar, Madan Puri

*Zulm Ki Pukar* (1979)
DIRECTOR: Ramnesh Puri
CAST: Ranjeeta Kaur, Parakshit Sahni, Amjad
Khan, Kader Khan, Madan Puri

*Radha Aur Seeta* (1979)
DIRECTOR: Vijay Kapoor
CAST: Arun Govil, Rita Bhaduri

*The Great Gambler* (1979)
DIRECTOR: Shakti Samanta
CAST: Amitabh Bacchan, Zeenat Amman, Neetu
Singh, Prem Chopra
CHARACTER: Ratan Das

*Gautam Govinda* (1979)
DIRECTOR: Subhas Ghai
CAST: Shashi Kapoor, Moushumi Chatterjee,
Shatrughan Sinha, Reena Roy, Prem Nath
CHARACTER: Bagha

*Aur Kaun?* (1979)
DIRECTOR: Ramsay Brothers
CAST: Sachin, Om Shivpuri, Roopesh Kumar

*Jaan-E-Bahaar....* (1979)
DIRECTOR: Prakash Kapoor
CAST: Sachin, Sarika, Asrani, Jagdeep
CHARACTER: Mama

*Jaani Dushman* (1979)
DIRECTOR: Raaj Kumar Kohli
CAST: Sunil Dutt, Sanjeev Kumar, Shatrughan
Sinha, Vinod Mehra, Prem Nath, Sarika, Reena
Roy, Rekha, Neetu Singh
CHARACTER: Blind Vaidji

*Jatt Punjabi (Punjabi)* (1979)
DIRECTOR: Satish Bhakri
CAST: Manoj Kumar, Raza Murad, Satish Kaul,
Meher Mittal, Rajendra Nath, Komila Virk

*Noorie* \*\*\* (1979)
DIRECTOR: Manmohan Krishna
CAST: Farooq Shaikh, Poonam Dhillon, Manmohan Krishna
CHARACTER: Karam

*Aakhri Kasam* (1979)
DIRECTOR: Ramnesh Puri
CAST: Vinod Mehra, Yogeeta Bali, Kabir Bedi

*Kaala Pathar* (1979)
DIRECTOR: Yash Chopra
CAST: Amitabh Bachchan, Rakhee, Rishi Kapoor, Neetu Singh, Shashi Kapoor, Shatrughan Sinha, Purveen Babi, Prem Chopra, Parikshit Sahni, Poonam Dhillon, Sanjeev Kumar, Manmohan Krishna

*Gawah* (1979)

*Zaalim* (1979)
DIRECTOR: Ram Singh
CAST: Vinod Khanna, Leena Chandarwarkar, Nirupa Roy, Rehman, Pran, Iftekhar, Keshto Mukherjee

*Bandhi* (1978)
DIRECTOR: Alo Sarkar
CAST: Uttam Kumar, Sulakshana Pandit, Amjad Khan, Amrish Puri

*Ghar* (1978)
DIRECTOR: Manik Chaterjee
CAST: Vinod Mehra, Rekha, Prema Narayan, Asrani
CHARACTER: Father

*Aahuti* (1978)
DIRECTOR: Ashok V Bhushan
CAST: Rajendra Kumar, Shashi Kapoor, Rakesh Roshan, Purveen Babi, Asha Sachdev, Kamini Kaushal
CHARACTER: Heeralal

*Ankhiyon Ke Jharokhon Se* (1978)
DIRECTOR: Hiren Nag
CAST: Sachin, Ranjeeta, Iftekhar, Urmila Bhatt
CHARACTER: Mr Mathur

*Chor Ho To Aisa* (1978)
DIRECTOR: Ravi Tandon
CAST: Shatrughan Sinha, Reena Roy, Pran, Bindu, Raza Murad
CHARACTER: Ramu

*Heeralal Pannalal* (1978)
DIRECTOR: Ashok Roy

CAST: Shashi Kapoor, Rishi Kapoor, Zeenat Aman, Neetu Singh, Ajit, Premnath, Ranjeet

*Naya Daur* (1978)
DIRECTOR: Mahesh Bhatt
CAST: Rishi Kapoor, Farida Jalal, Bhavna Bhatt, Danny, Om Prakash, Ranjeet

*Swarg Narak* (1978)
DIRECTOR: Narayan Rao Dasani
CAST: Sanjiv Kumar, Jeetendra, Vinod Mehra, Maushumi, Shabana Azmi, Tanuja, Jagdeep
CHARACTER: Lalchand

*Vishwanath* (1978)
DIRECTOR: Subhash Ghai
CAST: Shatrughan Sinha, Reena Roy, Rita Bhaduri, Parikshit Sahni, Pran, Prem Nath
CHARACTER: Pukhraj

*Jai Ambe Maa* (1977)
DIRECTOR: Jal
CAST: Dalpat,Shahu Modak, Anita Guha, Ashish Kumar

*Mandir Masjid* (1977)
DIRECTOR: Mohammed Hussein
CAST: Jagdeep, Yogita Bali, Nutan, Lalita Pawar, Dr Shreeram Lagoo

*Angarey* (1977)
DIRECTOR: Govind Saraiya
CAST: Sanjeev Kumar, Rakhee, Alka, Dheeraj Kumar

*Chaalu Mera Naam* (1977)
DIRECTOR: Krishna Naidu
CAST: Vinod Mehra, Vidya Sinha, Helen, Mahendra Sandhu

*Mera Vachan Geeta Ki Kasam* (1977)
DIRECTOR: Vinod Kumar
CAST: Saira Banu, Sanjay Khan

*Aaina* (1977)
DIRECTOR: K Bhalachander
CAST: Rajesh Khanna, Mumtaz, Manmohan Krishna
CHARACTER: M B Patil

*Chakkar Pe Chakkar* (1977)
DIRECTOR: Ashok Roy
CAST: Shashi Kapoor, Rekha, Pran

*Darinda* (1977)
DIRECTOR: Kaushal Bharati
CAST: Feroz Khan, Sunil Dutt, Purveen Babi, Prem Nath

*Dulhan Wohi Jo Piya Man Bhaye* (1977)
DIRECTOR: Lekh Tandon
CAST: Rameshwari, Prem Kishen, Iftikar, Shahsikala

*Kasam Khoon Ki* (1977)
DIRECTOR: Ashok Roy
CAST: Jeetendra, Sulakshana Pandit, Prem Chopra,
Aruna Irani, Amjad Khan

*Paapi* (1977)
DIRECTOR: O P Ralhan
CAST: Sunil Dutt, Sanjeev Kumar, Zeenat Aman,
Reena Roy, Prem Chopra
CHARACTER: Harnamdas

*Ram Bharose* (1977)
DIRECTOR: Anand Sagar
CAST: Randhir Kapoor, Rekha, Dara Singh

*Shirdi Ke Sai Baba* (1977)
DIRECTOR: Ashok V Bhushan
CAST: Sudhir Dalvi, Manoj Kumar, Rajendra
Kumar, Hema Malini, Manmohan Krishna
CHARACTER: Ranbir

*Vishwasghaat* (1977)
DIRECTOR: Mahesh Bhatt
CAST: Sanjeev Kumar, Shabana Azmi, Kabir Bedi
CHARACTER: Uday's Dad

*Vangaar (Punjabi)* (1977)
DIRECTOR: Prof Narula
CAST: Baldev Khosa, Vijay Tandon, Meena Rai,
Manmohan Krishna, Chaman Puri

*Lachhi* (1977)
DIRECTOR: Rajendra Sharma
CAST: Satish Kaul, Bhavna Bhatt, Raza Murad,
Mumtaz Begum, Madan Puri

*Sher Puttar* (1977)
DIRECTOR: Subhash Bhakri
CAST: Dheeraj Kumar, Padma Khanna, Manmohan
Krishna, Madan Puri

*Barood* (1976)
DIRECTOR: Pramod Chakraborty
CAST: Dharmendra, Hema Malini, Ashok Kumar,
Rishi Kapoor, Reena Roy, Ajit, Prem Chopra

*Deewangee* (1976)
DIRECTOR: Samir Ganguly
CAST: Shashi Kapoor, Zeenat Aman, Narendranath,
Madan Puri

*Fakira* \*\*\* (1976)
DIRECTOR: C P Dixit

CAST: Shashi Kapoor, Shabana Azmi, Danny,
Asrani, Aruna Irani, Iftekhar, Madan Puri
CHARACTER: Chiman Lal

*Mehbooba* (1976)
DIRECTOR: Shakti Samanta
CAST: Rajesh Khanna, Hema Malini, Prem Chopra,
Manmohan Krishna
CHARACTER: Sardar

*Bhanwar* (1976)
DIRECTOR: Bhapie Sonie
CAST: Ashok Kumar, Randhir Kapoor, Parveen
Babi
CHARACTER: D'Souza

*Aaj Ka Ye Ghar* (1976)
DIRECTOR: Surinder Shailaj
CAST: Romesh Sharma, Jaymala, I S Johar,
Chandrashekar, Lalita Pawar, Madan Puri
CHARACTER: Father-in-law

*Aap Beeti* (1976)
DIRECTOR: Mohan Kumar
CAST: Shashi Kapoor, Hema Malini, Ashok Kumar

*Bairaag* (1976)
DIRECTOR: Asit Sen
CAST: Dilip Kumar, Saira Banu

*Daaj* (1976)
DIRECTOR: Dharam Kumar
CAST: Dheeeraj Kumar, Jeevan

*Kalicharan* (1976)
DIRECTOR: Subhash Ghai
CAST: Shatrughan Sinha, Reena Roy
CHARACTER: Jaagir

*Khalifa* (1976)
DIRECTOR: Prakash Mehra
CAST: Randhir Kapoor, Rekha, Pran

*Dharmatma* (1975)
DIRECTOR: Feroz Khan
CAST: Feroz Khan, Hema Malini, Rekha, Danny

*Zameer* (1975)
DIRECTOR: Ravi Chopra
CAST: Amitabh Bachhan, Saira Banu, Shammi
Kapoor
CHARACTER: Maan Singh

*Dafaa 302* (1975)
DIRECTOR: K Srivastava
CAST: Ashok Kumar, Randhir Kapoor, Rekha
CHARACTER: I G Police

*Deewaar* (1975)
DIRECTOR: Yash Chopra
CAST: Amitabh Bachhan, Shashi Kapoor, Nirupa Roy, Purveen Babi, Nitu Singh, Madan Puri
CHARACTER: Samant

*Geet Gaata Chal* (1975)
DIRECTOR: Hiren Nag
CAST: Sachin, Sarika, Urmila Bhat
CHARACTER: Sohan Singh

*Ponga Pandit* (1975)
DIRECTOR: Prayag Raj
CAST: Randhir Kapoor, Neeta Mehta, Danny, Prema Narayan
CHARACTER: Shambhu

*Rafoo Chakkar* \*\*\* (1975)
DIRECTOR: Narinder Bedi
CAST: Rishi Kapoor, Neetu Singh
CHARACTER: Prakash

*Raftaar* (1975)
DIRECTOR: Ramnesh Puri
CAST: Vinod Mehra, Moushumi Chatterjee, Danny, Ranjit
CHARACTER: Rita's dad

*Saazish* (1975)
DIRECTOR: Kalidas
CAST: Dharmendra, Saira Banu

*Warrant* (1975)
DIRECTOR: Pramod Chakraborty
CAST: Dev Anand, Zeenat Aman, Pran
CHARACTER: Professor Verma

*Morni* (1975)
DIRECTOR: Jugal Kishore
CAST: Satish Kaul, Radha Saluja, Madan Puri

*Aaina* (1974)
DIRECTOR: K Balachandra
CAST: Rajesh Khanna, Dharmendra, Kamal Hussein, Neetu Singh, Mumtaz, Manmohan Krishna

*Charitraheen* (1974)
DIRECTOR: Shakti Samanta
CAST: Sanjeev Kumar, Sharmila Tagore, Parveen Babi, Yogeeta Bali

*Chhatis Ghante* (1974)
DIRECTOR: Raj Tilak
CAST: Sunil Dutt, Mala Sinha, Vijay Arora, Parveen Babi

*Sauda* (1974)
DIRECTOR: Sudesh Issar

*Majboor* (1974)
DIRECTOR: Ravi Tandon
CAST: Amitabh Bachchan, Parveen Babi, Pran
CHARACTER: Mahipat Rai

*Benaam* (1974)
DIRECTOR: Narendra Bedi
CAST: Amitabh Bachchan, Moushumi Chatterjee, I
CHARACTER: Gopal

*Ajanabee* (1974)
DIRECTOR: Shakti Samanta
CAST: Rajesh Khanna, Zeenat Aman, Prem Chopra, Manmohan Krishna
CHARACTER: Mr Puri

*Jab Andhera Hota Hai* (1974)
DIRECTOR: Deepak Bahri
CAST: Vikram, Prema Narayan, Jala Agha, Prem Chopra, Helen, Sajjan, Madan Puri

*Chor Machaye Shor* (1974)
DIRECTOR: N N Sippy
CAST: Shashi Kapoor, Mumtaz, Danny, Asrani, Asit Sen, Madan Puri
CHARACTER: Jamunadas

*Bidaai* (1974)
DIRECTOR: L V Prasad
CAST: Jeetendra, Leena Chandravarkar

*Manoranjan* \*\*\* (1974)
DIRECTOR: Shammi Kapoor
CAST: Shammi Kapoor, Sanjeev Kumar, Zeenat Aman
CHARACTER: Inspector

*Pran Jaye Par Vachan Na Jaye* (1974)
DIRECTOR: Ali Raza
CAST: Sunil Dutt, Rekha, Ranjit, Prem Nath
CHARACTER: Jagmohan

*Roti Kapada Aur Makaan* (1974)
DIRECTOR: Manoj Kumar
CAST: Manoj Kumar, Amitabh Bacchan, Shashi Kapoor, Zeenat Aman, Moushumi Chaterjee
CHARACTER: Nekiram

*Zehreela Insaan* (1974)
DIRECTOR: S R Puttana Kangal
CAST: Rishi Kapoor, Maushumi Chatterjee, Neetu Singh

*Badla* (1974)
DIRECTOR: Vijay
CAST: Shatrugan Sinha, Moushumi Chatterjee, Ajit, Mehmood, Raj Mehra, Anwar Hussein, Alka, Mac Mohan, Nirupa Roy, Shetty, Sunder, Meena T, Johnny Walker

*Daaman Aur Aag* (1973)
DIRECTOR: Vinod Kumar
CAST: Saira Banu, Sanjay Khan, Balraj Sahni, K N Singh

*Ek Nari Do Roop* (1973)
CAST: Roopesh Kumar, Shatrughan Sinha, Nadira

*Hifazat* (1973)
DIRECTOR: K S R Das
CAST: Ashok Kumar, Vinod Mehra, Asha Sachdev

*Kahani Hum Sub Ki* (1973)
DIRECTOR: Raj Kumar Kohli
CAST: Roopesh Kumar, Mala Sinha

*Wohi Raat Wohi Aawaz* (1973)
DIRECTOR: Dev Kishen
CAST: Sohnia Sahni, Sujit Kumar, Manmohan Krishna

*Joshila* (1973)
DIRECTOR: Yash Chopra
CAST: Dev Anand, Hema Malini, Pran, Manmohan Krishna

*Loafer* (1973)
DIRECTOR: A Bhimsingh
CAST: Dharmendar, Mumtaz

*Dhund* (1973)
DIRECTOR: B R Chopra
CAST: Sanjay Khan, Zeenat Aman, Danny, Ashok Kumar, Navin Nischal
CHARACTER: Inspector

*Bada Kabutar* (1973)
DIRECTOR: Devan Verma
CAST: Ashok Kumar, Amitabh Bachchan, Rehana Sultan
CHARACTER: Ghaffoor

*Bandhe Haath* (1973)
DIRECTOR: O P Goyal
CAST: Amitabh Bacchan, Mumtaz
CHARACTER: Mentor

*Daag* (1973)
DIRECTOR: Yash Chopra
CAST: Sharmila Tagore, Rajesh Khanna, Rakhee, Manmohan Krishna, Iftekhar, Karan Dewan, Kader Khan, Madan Puri
CHARACTER: K C Khanna

*Dharma* (1973)
DIRECTOR: Chand
CAST: Navin Nischol, Rekha, Pran, Sonia Sahni, Chandrashekar, Murad, Madan Puri
CHARACTER: Mangal Singh

*Gaddaar* (1973)
DIRECTOR: Harmesh Malhotra
CAST: Vinod Khanna, Yogeeta Bali, Pran, Manmohan, Anwar Hussein, Ifthekar, Madan Puri

*Nafrat* (1973)
DIRECTOR: Shyam Ralhan
CAST: Rakesh Roshan, Yogeeta Bali, Prem Chopra

*Black Mail* (1973/I)
Vijay Anand
CAST: Dharmendra, Rakhee, Shatrughan Sinha
CHARACTER: Khurana

*Naya Nasha* (1973)
DIRECTOR: Hari Dutt
CAST: Sharad Kumar, Nanda, Ranjeet, Manmohan Krishna

*Khoon Khoon* (1973)
DIRECTOR: Mohammed Hussein
CAST: Rekha, Mahendra Sandhu, Danny, Jagdeep, Faryal, Helen, Agha, Padma Khanna, Karan Dewan , Murad, Madan Puri

*Pattola* (1973)
DIRECTOR: Harish Rana
CAST: Indira Billi, Raj Oberoi, Sunder, Madan Puri

*Bandagi* (1972)
DIRECTOR: K Shankar
CAST: Vinod Mehra, Sandhya Rao

*Shezada* (1972)
DIRECTOR: K Shankar
CAST: Rajesh Khanna, Rakhi, Veena, Karan Dewan, Pandari Bai, P Jairaj

*Rut Rangeelee Aayee* (1972)
DIRECTOR: M M Pushkarna
CAST: Shyama, Rehman, Ramesh Deo

*Anuraag* (1972)
DIRECTOR: Shakti Samantha
CAST: Ashok Kumar, Rajesh Khanna, Moushami, Nutan, Vinod Mehra
CHARACTER: Amirchand

*Apna Desh* (1972)
DIRECTOR: Jambu
CAST: Rajesh Khanna, Jaya Pradha, Mumtaz, Om Prakash, Manmohan Krishna
CHARACTER: Narayan

*Apradh* (1972)
DIRECTOR: Feroz Khan
CAST: Feroz Khan, Mumtaz, Prem Chopra
CHARACTER: German

*Dastaan* (1972)
DIRECTOR: B R Chopra
CAST: Dilip Kumar, Sharmila Tagore,Manmohan Krishna

*Double Cross* (1972)
DIRECTOR: Gogi Anand
CAST: Vijay Anand, Rekha, Dev Kumar, Asha Sachdev, Madan Puri
CHARACTER: Maganbhai

*Gora Aur Kala* (1972)
DIRECTOR: Naresh Kumar
CAST: Rajendra Kumar, Hema Malini, Rekha, Prem Nath, Prem Chopra, Jagdeep, Sunder, Ram Mohan,Kamal Kapoor, Rajan Haksar, Dev Kumar, Madan Puri
CHARACTER: Zohravar Singh

*Haar Jeet* (1972)
DIRECTOR: C P Dixit
CAST: Rehana Sultana, Radha Saluja, Anil Dhawan, Mehmood, Sarika, Kamini Kaushal, Madan Puri

*Janwar Aur Insaan* (1972)
DIRECTOR: Tapi Chanakya
CAST: Shashi Kapoor, Rakhee, Shabnam, Sujit Kumar, Jagdeep, Nirupa Roy, Madan Puri

*Rani Mera Naam* (1972)
DIRECTOR: K S R Doss
CAST: Vijayalalitha, Anwar, Nazir Hussein, Natraj, Iftekhar, Jagdeep, Ashok Kumar, Premnath, Madan Puri

*Samadhi* (1972)
DIRECTOR: Prakash Mehra
CAST: Dharmendra, Asha Parekh, Jaya Bhaduri, Vijay Arora, Abhi Bhattacharya, Leela Mishra, Madan Puri

*Sazaa* (1972)
DIRECTOR: Chand
CAST: Kabir Bedi, Yogeeta Bali, Jeetendra, Rekha, Pran, Ashok Kumar, Rajendranath, Helen, Madan Puri

*Shehzada* (1972)
DIRECTOR: K Shankar
CAST: Rajesh Khanna, Rakhee, Karan Diwan, Pandharibai
CHARACTER: Mamaji

*Shor* (1972)
DIRECTOR: Manoj Kumar
CAST: Manoj Kumar, Jaya Bhaduri, Premnath, Kamini Kaushal

*Wafaa* (1972)
DIRECTOR: Ramanna
CAST: Sanjay Khan, Rakhee, Premnath
CHARACTER: Zamindar

*Jai Jwala* (1972)
DIRECTOR: Manohar Deepak
CAST: Sunil Dutt, Sujit Kumar, Ram Mohan, Dinesh Hingoo

*Jaane Bahar* (1972)

*Bahake Kadam* (1971)
DIRECTOR: Dharmesh Datt
CAST: Roopesh Kumar, Aparajita, Agha, Nadira

*Ek Paheli* (1971)
DIRECTOR: Naresh Kumar
CAST: Feroze Khan, Tanuja, Sanjeev Kumar, Prem Nath

*Nadaan* (1971)
DIRECTOR: Devan Verma
CAST: Asha Parekh, Navin Nischol
CHARACTER: Manghu

*Purani Pehchan* (1971)
DIRECTOR: Sohanlal Kanwar
CAST: Manoj Kumar, Babita, Balraj Sahni

*Amar Prem* (1971)
DIRECTOR: Shakti Samanta
CAST: Rajesh Khanna, Sharmila, Vinod Mehra
CHARACTER: Nepali

*Caravan* (1971)
DIRECTOR: Nasir Hussain
CAST: Jeetendra, Asha Parekh
CHARACTER: Mithalal

*Elaan* (1971)
DIRECTOR: F C Mehra
CAST: Rekha, Vinod Mehra, Vinod Khanna
CHARACTER: Mr Verma

*Haathi Mere Saathi* (1971)
DIRECTOR: M A Thirumugam

CAST: Rajesh Khanna, Tanuja, K N Singh
CHARACTER: Ratanlal

*Hulchul* (1971)
DIRECTOR: O P Ralhan
CAST: Kabir Bedi, Zeenat Aman
CHARACTER: Mahesh

*Lakhon Mein Ek* (1971)
DIRECTOR: S S Balan
CAST: Jalal Agha, Radha, Pran
CHARACTER: Jaggu

*Paras* (1971)
DIRECTOR: C P Dixit
CAST: Sanjeev Kumar, Rakhee, Shatrughan Sinha
CHARACTER: Thakur

*Rakhwala* (1971)
DIRECTOR: A Subba Rao
CAST: Dharmendra, Vinod Khanna, Rakesh Pandey, Leena Chandraverkar

*Ramu Ustad* (1971)
DIRECTOR: Mohammed Hussein
CAST: Dara Singh, Jayshree T

*Sanjog* (1971)
DIRECTOR: S S Balan
CAST: Amitabh Bachchan, Mala Singh
CHARACTER: Shiv Dayal

*Woh Din Yaad Karo* (1971)
DIRECTOR: K Amarnath
CAST: Sanjay, Nanda

*The Train* (1971)
DIRECTOR: Ravikant Nagaich
CAST: Rajesh Khanna, Nanda, Chaman Puri
CHARACTER: No. 1

*Aag Aur Daag* (1970)
DIRECTOR: A Salaam
CAST: Joy Mukherjee, Zeb Rehman

*Bhai Bhai* (1970)
DIRECTOR: Raja Nawathe
CAST: Sunil Dutt, Asha Parekh, Mumtaz, Pran, Manmohan Krishna

*Araadhana* (1970)
DIRECTOR: Shakti Samanta
CAST: Rajesh Khanna, Sharmila Tagore
CHARACTER: Warden

*Choron Ka Chor* (1970)
DIRECTOR: Mohammed Hussein
CAST: Dara Singh, Shabnam

*Devi* (1970)
DIRECTOR: R V Madhusudan
CAST: Sanjiv Kumar, Nutan, Rehman, Manmohan Krishna
CHARACTER: Joginder

*Kati Patang* (1970)
DIRECTOR: Shakti Samantha
CAST: Rajesh Khanna, Asha Parekh, Prem Chopra
CHARACTER: Vishnu

*My Love* (1970)
DIRECTOR: S Sukhdev
CAST: Shashi Kapoor, Sharmila Tagore

*Prem Pujari* (1970)
DIRECTOR: Dev Anand
CAST: Dev Anand, Waheeda Rehman, Shatrughan Sinha
CHARACTER: Chang

*Purab Aur Pachhim* (1970)
DIRECTOR: Manoj Kumar
CAST: Manoj Kumar, Saira Banu, Pran, Ashok Kumar, Prem Chopra, Madan Puri

*Yaadgaar* (1970)
DIRECTOR: S Ram Sharma
CAST: Manoj Kumar, Nutan, Pran, Prem Chopra, Kamini Kaushal
CHARACTER: Madan

*Ehsaan* (1970)
DIRECTOR: Shiv Kumar
CAST: Joy Mukherjee, Anjana Mumtaz, K N Singh
CHARACTER: Pawan

*Harishchandra Taramati* (1970)
DIRECTOR: B K Adarsh
CAST: Pradip Kumar, Shyama, Helen, Tiwari, Jayshree T, Jeevan, Sapru, Manorama, Madhumati, B M Vyas, Tun Tun, Madan Puri

*Ittefaq* (1969)
DIRECTOR: Yash Chopra
CAST: Rajesh Khanna, Nanda
CHARACTER: Prosecutor

*Aadmi Aur Insaan* (1969)
DIRECTOR: Yash Chopra
CAST: Dharmendra, Saira Banu, Feroz Khan, Mumtaz
CHARACTER: Sabharwal

*Pyar Hi Pyar* (1969)
DIRECTOR: Bhappi Sonie

CAST: Dharmendra, Vyjantimala, Pran
CHARACTER: Dindayal

*Pyar Ka Mausam* (1969)
DIRECTOR: Nasir Hussain
CAST: Shashi Kapoor, Asha Parekh
CHARACTER: Shankar

*Shatranj* (1969)
DIRECTOR: S S Vasan
CAST: Rajendra Kumar, Waheeda Rehman,
Mehmood, Agha, Manmohan Krishna
CHARACTER: Chang

*Talash* (1969)
DIRECTOR: O P Ralhan
CAST: Rajendra Kumar, Sharmila Tagore, Balraj Sahni
CHARACTER: Peter

*Jaalsaaz* (1969)
DIRECTOR: Mohammed Hussein
CAST: Kishore Kumar, Mala Sinha, Pran

*Saajan* (1969)
DIRECTOR: Mohan Sehgal
CAST: Manoj Kumar, Asha Parekh, Shatrughan
Sinha

*Shart* (1969)
DIRECTOR: Kewal Mishra
CAST: Sanjay Khan, Mumtaz, K N Singh

*Tumse Achcha Kaun Hai* (1969)
DIRECTOR: Pramod Chakravorty
CAST: Shammi Kapoor, Babita, Pran

*Aankhen* (1968)
DIRECTOR: Ramanand Sagar
CAST: Dharmendra, Mala Sinha
CHARACTER: Captain

*Duniya* (1968)
DIRECTOR: T Prakash Rao
CAST: Dev Anand, Vyjantimala, Balraj Sahni,
Prem Chopra

*Hai Mera Dil* (1968)
DIRECTOR: Ved-Madan
CAST: Kishore Kumar, Kumkum

*Hamsaya* (1968)
DIRECTOR: Joy Mukherjee
CAST: Joy Mukherjee, Mala Sinha, Sharmila
Tagore, Rehman

*Juaari* (1968)
DIRECTOR: Suraj Prakash
CAST: Shashi Kapoor, Nanda, Tanuja, Rehman

*Aanchal Ke Phool* (1968)
DIRECTOR: Karunesh Thakore
CAST: Kamini Kaushal, Sajjan, Chand Usmani

*Ek Phool Ek Bhool* (1968)
DIRECTOR: Kedar Kapoor
CAST: Sudhir, Jeb Rehman, K N Singh

*Kahin Aur Chal* (1968)
DIRECTOR: Vijay Anand
CAST: Dev Anand, Asha Parekh

*Teri Talash Mein* (1968)
DIRECTOR: Vinod Talwar
CAST: Rita Bhaduri, Krishna, Sudhir Pandey

*Aag* (1967)
DIRECTOR: Naresh Kumar
CAST: Feroz Khan, Mumtaz, Shyama
CHARACTER: Kallu Singh

*Aamne Samne* (1967)
DIRECTOR: Suraj Prakash
CAST: Shashi Kapoor, Sharmila Tagore, Prem
Chopra

*Baharon Ke Sapne* (1967)
DIRECTOR: Nasir Hussein
CAST: Rajesh Khanna, Asha Parekh, Prem Nath

*Gunehgar* (1967)
DIRECTOR: Sheikh Mukhtiar
CAST: Sanjeev Kumar, Kumkum

*Hamraaz* \*\*\* (1967)
DIRECTOR: B R Chopra
CAST: Sunil Dutt, Raaj Kumar, Vimi, Balraj Sahni,
Mumtaz,Manmohan Krishna
CHARACTER: Captain

*Johar in Bombay* (1967)
DIRECTOR: I S Johar
CAST: Johar, Sonia

*Shagird* (1967)
DIRECTOR: Samir Ganguli
CAST: Joy Mukherjee, Saira Banu, I S Johar
CHARACTER: Madan

*Upkaar* (1967)
DIRECTOR: Manoj Kumar
CAST: Manoj Kumar, Saira Banu, Pran, Kamini
Kaushal, Prem Chopra, Manmohan Krishna
CHARACTER: Charan Das

*Dilruba* (1967)
DIRECTOR: Mohammed Hussein
CAST: Kumkum, Shyam Kumar

*Ek Raat* (1967)
DIRECTOR: Raj Nath
CAST: Sheikh Mukhtar, Shyama, Simi Garewal

*Hamare Gamse Mat Khelo* (1967)
DIRECTOR: Pal Premi
CAST: Bharati Devi, Raza Murad

*Nasihat* (1967)
DIRECTOR: Om Patwar
CAST: Dara Singh, Helen

*Dil Ruba* (1967)
DIRECTOR: Mohammed Hussein
CAST: Ajit, Kumkum

*Evening in Paris* \*\*\* (1966)
DIRECTOR: Shakti Samantha
CAST: Shammi Kapoor, Sharmila Tagore, Pran

*Love in Tokyo* (1966)
DIRECTOR: Pramod Chakraborty
CAST: Joy Mukherji, Asha Parekh, Pran

*Main Wohi Hoon* (1966)
DIRECTOR: A Shamsheer
CAST: Feroze Khan, Kumkum

*Phool Aur Patthar* (1966)
DIRECTOR: O P Ralhan
CAST: Dharminder, Meena Kumari, Manmohan Krishna

*Sawan Ki Ghata* (1966)
DIRECTOR: Shakti Samanta
CAST: Manoj Kumar, Sharmila Tagore, Pran

*Th. Jarnail Singh* (1966)
DIRECTOR: Mohammed Hussein
CAST: Dara Singh, Sheikh Mukhtiar, Helen

*Yeh Zindagi Kitni Haseen Hai* (1966)
DIRECTOR: R K Nayyar
CAST: Joy Mukherjee, Saira Bano, Ashok Kumar

*Do Matwale* (1966)
DIRECTOR: Kamran
CAST: Helen, Kamran

*Main Wohi Hoon* (1966)
DIRECTOR: A Shamsheer
CAST: Feroz Khan, Kumkum

*Naujawan* (1966)
DIRECTOR: Chand
CAST: Dara Singh, Nishi, Chaman Puri

*Street Singer* (1966)
DIRECTOR: Chandrashekar
CAST: Chandrashekar, Sarita, Manmohan Krishna

*Gumnaam* (1965)
DIRECTOR: Raja Nawathe
CAST: Manoj Kumar, Nanda, Pran

*Mohabbat Isko Kahete Hain* (1965)
DIRECTOR: Akhtar Mirza
CAST: Shashi Kapoor, Nanda

*Neela Aakash* (1965)
DIRECTOR: Rajendra Bhatia
CAST: Dharmendra, Mala Sinha

*Shaheed* (1965)
DIRECTOR: Manoj Kumar
CAST: Manoj Kumar, Pran

*Waqt* (1965)
DIRECTOR: Yash Chopra
CAST: Raj Kumar, Shashi Kapoor, Sadhana, Sharmila Tagore, Balraj Sahni, Madan
CHARACTER: Balbir

*Main Hoon Alladin* (1965)
DIRECTOR: Mohammed Hussein
CAST: Ajit, Sayeeda Khan

*Flight to Assam* (1965)
DIRECTOR: Ranjan, Shashikala

*Tel Maalish* (1965)
DIRECTOR: Romney Dey
CAST: Sheikh Mukhtar, Kumkum

*Bombay Race Course* (1965)
DIRECTOR: Kedar Kapoor
CAST: Ajit, Nalini

*Ayee Milan Ki Bela*\*\*\* (1964)
DIRECTOR: J Om Prakash
CAST: Rajendra Kumar, Saira Baanu, Dharmendra
CHARACTER: Ratanlal

*Cha Cha Cha* (1964)
DIRECTOR: Chandrashekar
CAST: Chandrashekar, Helen

*Kashmir Ki Kali* (1964)
DIRECTOR: Shakti Samantha
CAST: Shammi Kapoor, Sharmila Tagore
CHARACTER: Shyamlal

*Kohra* (1964)
DIRECTOR: Biren Nag
CAST: Biswajeet, Waheeda Rehman, Manmohan Krishna

*Mr. X in Bombay* (1964)
DIRECTOR: Shantilal Soni
CAST: Kishore Kumar, Kumkum

*Shakshi Gopal* (1964)
DIRECTOR: Balu Bhai
CAST: Bharat Bhushan, Nanda

*Ziddi* (1964)
DIRECTOR: Pramod Chakraborty
CAST: Joy Mukherjee, Asha Parekh
CHARACTER: Moti

*Main Jatti Punjab di* (1964)
DIRECTOR: Baldev Jhingon
CAST: Nishi, Jeevan, Tun Tun, Bhangeshah

*Dekha Pyar Tumhara* (1963)
DIRECTOR: Kalpatru
CAST: Subi Raj, Naaz, Madan Puri

*Ek Raaz* (1963)
DIRECTOR: Shakti Samantha
CAST: Kishore Kumar, Jamuna, Pran

*Gehra Daag* (1963)
DIRECTOR: O P Ralhan
CAST: Rajendra Kumar, Mala Sinha, Manmohan Krishna

*Godaan* (1963)
DIRECTOR: Trilok Jetley
CAST: Raaj Kumar, Kamini Kaushal

*Shikari* (1963)
DIRECTOR: Mohammed Hussein
CAST: Ajit, Ragini

*Sunheri Nagin* (1963)
DIRECTOR: Babubhai Mistry
CAST: Ajit, Ragini

*Naughty Boy* (1962)
DIRECTOR: Shakti Samantha
CAST: Kishore Kumar, Kalpana

*Dr. Vidya* (1962)
DIRECTOR: Rajinder Bhatia
CAST: Manoj Kumar, Vyjantimala

*Gangu Dada* (1962)
DIRECTOR: Pramod Chakraborty
CAST: Sheikh Mukhtar, Naaz

*Kala Chashma* (1962)
DIRECTOR: K Vinod
CAST: Manju, Amarnath

*Bees Saal Baad* (1962)
DIRECTOR: Biren Nag
CAST: Biswajeet, Waheeda Rehman, Manmohan Krishna
CHARACTER: Dr Pandey

*China Town* (1962)
DIRECTOR: Shakti Samantha
CAST: Shammi Kapoor, Sharmila Tagore

*Rakhi* (1962)
DIRECTOR: A Bhim Singh
CAST: Pradeep Kumar, Ameeta

*Modern Girl* (1961)
DIRECTOR: R Bhattacharya
CAST: Pradeep Kumar, Nimmi, Sayeeda Khan

*Saaya* (1961)
DIRECTOR: Shiriram Bohra
CAST: Nasir Khan, Nigar Sultana

*Tel Malish Boot Polish* (1961)
DIRECTOR: Romney Dey
CAST: Chandrashekhar, Kumkum

*Pyaar Ka Saagar* (1961)
DIRECTOR: Devendra Goel
CAST: Rajendra Kumar, Meena Kumari

*Guddi* (*Punjabi*) (1961)
DIRECTOR: Jugal Kishore
CAST: Diljeet, Nishi, Wast

*Ghar ki Laaj* (1960)
DIRECTOR: V M Vyas
CAST: Nirupa Roy

*Chaudhary Karnail Singh* (*Punjabi*) (1960)
DIRECTOR: Krishan Kumar
CAST: Jagdish Sethi, Prem Chopra, Krishna Kumari
CHARACTER: Boota Singh

*Jaali Note* \*\*\* (1960)
DIRECTOR: Shakti Samantha
CAST: Dev Anand, Madhubala

*Kalaa Bazar* (1960)
DIRECTOR: Vijay Anand
CAST: Dev Anand, Waheeda Rehman, Nanda, Vijay Anand, Chetan Anand, Guru Dutt, Geeta Dutt, Naseem Banu, Dilip Kumar, Raaj Kumar, Rajinder Kumar
CHARACTER: Ganesh

*Kiklee* (*Punjabi*) (1960)
DIRECTOR: Bekal Amritsari
CAST: Jagdish Sethi Indra Bansal, Madhumati

*Singapore* (1960)
DIRECTOR: Shakti Samantha
CAST: Shammi Kapoor, Padmini
CHARACTER: Chang

*Gambler* (1960)
DIRECTOR: Dwarka Khosla
CAST: Prem Nath, Shakila, Pran

*Insaan Jaag Utha* (1959)
DIRECTOR: Shakti Samantha
CAST: Sunil Dutt, Madhubala
CHARACTER: Mohan Singh

*Nai Raahen* (1959)
DIRECTOR: Brij
CAST: Ashok Kumar, Geeta Bali

*Charnon Ki Dasi* (1959)
DIRECTOR: Ramesh Vyas
CAST: Nirupa Roy, Manhar Desai

*Chirag Kahan Roshni Kahan* (1959)
DIRECTOR: Devendra Goel
CAST: Rajendra Kumar, Meena Kumari

*Amar Shaheed* (1959)
DIRECTOR: Ramakrishnaih Panthalu
CAST: Jagirdar
CHARACTER: Jagirdar

*Kanhaiya* (1959)
DIRECTOR: Om Prakash
CAST: Raj Kapoor, Nutan, Lalita Pawar, Raj Mehra, Nazir Huseein, Jagdish Sethi, Uma Dutt, Vishwas Mishra, Madan Puri

*Guddi* (1958)
DIRECTOR: K K Dewan
CAST: Daljit, Nishi, Wasti
CHARACTER: Lambhardar

*Dilli Ka Thug* (1958)
DIRECTOR: S D Narang
CAST: Nutan, Kishore Kumar

*Howrah Bridge* (1958)
DIRECTOR: Shakti Samantha
CAST: Ashok Kumar, Madhubal
CHARACTER: John Chang

*Kabhi Andhera Kabhi Ujala* (1958)
DIRECTOR: C P Dixit
CAST: Kishore Kumar, Nutan

*Taqdeer* (1958)
DIRECTOR: A S Chopra
CAST: Karan Dewan, Shyama

*Trolley Driver* (1958)
DIRECTOR: Gajanan Jagirdar
CAST: Bhagwan, Suraiya

*Balyogi Upmanyu* (1958)
DIRECTOR: H j Bhatt
CAST: Nirupa Roy, Vinod Kumar

*Miss 1958* (1958)
DIRECTOR: Kuldeep Kahar
CAST: Suraiya, Karan Dewan

*Narsi Bhagat* (1957)
DIRECTOR: Devendra Goel
CAST: Shahu Modak, Nirupa Roy

*Mirza Saheban* (1957)
DIRECTOR: Ravi Kapoor
CAST: Shammi Kapoor, Shyama
CHARACTER: Shamir

*Sheroo* (1957)
DIRECTOR: Paacchi
CAST: Ashok Kumar, Nalini Jaywant

*Baarish* (1957)
DIRECTOR: S Mukherjee
CAST: Dev Anand, Nutan

*Ek Saal* (1957)
DIRECTOR: Devendra Goel
CAST: Ashok Kumar, Madhubala

*Nau Do Gyarah* (1957)
DIRECTOR: Vijay Anand
CAST: Dev Anand, Kalpana Kartik
CHARACTER: Radhey

*Mohini* (1957)
DIRECTOR: Raman B Desai
CAST: Nirupa Roy, Shahu Modhak

*Sakshi Gopal* (1957)
DIRECTOR: Bhalchandra Shukla &Ramnik Vaidya
CAST: Bharat Bhushan, Nanda, Chaman Puri

*Kala Chor* (1956)
DIRECTOR: R C Kapoor
CAST: Amarnath, Chitra

*Aabroo* (1956)
DIRECTOR: Chatarbhuj Doshi
CAST: Kamini Kaushal, Kishore Kumar

*Heer (film)* (1956)
DIRECTOR: Hamid Bhutt
CAST: Nutan, Pradip Kumar, Chaman Puri, S L Puri

*Qeemat* (1956)
DIRECTOR: Hira Singh
CAST: Rehana Sultana, Abhi Bhattacharya

*Rukhsana* (1955)
DIRECTOR: R C Talwar
CAST: Meena Kumari, Kishore Kumar

*Miss 1955* (1955)
DIRECTOR: Kuldeep
CAST: Karan, Suraiya

*Bhagwat Mahima* (1955)
DIRECTOR: Vithaldas Panchotia
CAST: Ashok Kumar, Kishore Kumar, Nimmi, Shyama

*Jhanak Jhanak Payal Baaje\*\*\** (1955)
DIRECTOR: V Shanataram
CAST: Gopi Kishen, Sandhya, K Date, Chaman Puri, Madan Puri
CHARACTER: Madan Babu

*Madhur Milan* (1955)
DIRECTOR: Punwani
CAST: Mahipal, Roopmala

*Teen Bhai* (1955)
DIRECTOR: Hemchander Chunder
CAST: Nirupa Roy, Pahari Sanyal

*Tees Maar khan* (1955)
DIRECTOR: Kwatra
CAST: Agha, Shyama

*Ashatali* (1954)
DIRECTOR: Shanti Prakash Bakshi

*Watan* (1954)
DIRECTOR: Nana Bhai
CAST: Tirlok Kapoor, Nirupa Roy

*Haar-Jeet* (1954)
DIRECTOR: Jaggi Rampal
CAST: Shyama, Suresh, Sunder, Manorma, Sham Lal, Hira Lal, Madan Puri

*Munna* (1954)
DIRECTOR: K Abbas
CAST: David, Sulochna Chatterjee

*Shri Chaitanya Mahaprabhu* (1953)
DIRECTOR: Vijay Bhatt
CAST: Bharat Bhushan, Ameeta

*Diwaana* (1952)
DIRECTOR: A R Kardar
CAST: Suraiya, Suresh

*Goonj* (1952)
DIRECTOR: Phani Majumdar
CAST: Suresh, Suraiya, Chaman Puri

*Jaggu* (1952)
DIRECTOR: Jagdish Sethi
CAST: Shyama, Kamal Kapoor

*Raag Rang* (1952)
DIRECTOR: Bali
CAST: Ashok Kumar, Geeta Bali

*Zakhmi* (1952)
CAST: Jagirdar, Suraiya, Rehman

*Adaa* (1951)
DIRECTOR: D C Goel
CAST: Rehana, Shekhar

*Nadaan* (1951)
DIRECTOR: Hira Singh
CAST: Dev Anand, Madhu Bala

*Balo* (1951)
DIRECTOR: Kuldeep
CAST: Geeta Bali, Kuldeep Kaur, Arjun, Madan Puri

*Nazaria* (1950)
DIRECTOR: P L Santoshi
CAST: Sajjan, Geeta Bali

*Birha Ki Raat* (1950)
DIRECTOR: Gajanan Jagirdar
CAST: Dev Anand, Nargis

*Anmol Ratan* (1950)
DIRECTOR: M Sadiq
CAST: Karan Dewan, Meena Shorey

*Najariya* (1950)
DIRECTOR: P L Santoshi
CAST: Radhakishan, Mumtaz Ali, Sajjan, Harun

*Madari* (1950)
DIRECTOR: Rajendra Sharma
CAST: Shyama, Meena Shorey, Kuldeep Kaur, Suresh, Om Prakash, Madan Puri

*Raat ki Raani* (1949)
DIRECTOR: Jagdish Sethi
CAST: Shyam, Munnawar Sultana

*Dil Ki Duniya* (1949)
DIRECTOR: Mazar Khan
CAST: Geeta Bali, Munnawar Sultana

*Jeet* (1949)
DIRECTOR: Mohan Sinha
CAST: Dev Anand, Suraiya, Suraiya Choudhary, Madan Puri

*Phuman* (1949)
DIRECTOR: Rajpal

CAST: Kamal Kapoor, Geeta Bali

*Usha Kiran* (1949)
DIRECTOR: Shanti Bhai

*Namoona* (1949)
DIRECTOR: Hira Singh
CAST: Dev Anand, Kamini Kaushal
CHARACTER: Lacchu

*Singaar* (1949)
DIRECTOR: J K Nanda
CAST: Jairaj, Suraiya

*Imtehaan* (1949)
DIRECTOR: Mohan Sinha
CAST: Surendra, Tasneem

*Kamal* (1949)
DIRECTOR: Sonny Benjamin
CAST: Surendra, Naintara

*Sona* (1948)
DIRECTOR: Mazhar Khan
CAST: Madan Puri, Munnawar Sultana

*Vidya* (1948)
DIRECTOR: Girish Trivedi
CAST: Dev Anand, Suraiya
CHARACTER: Harilal

*Laakhon men Ek* (1947)
DIRECTOR: Hira lal
CAST: Raaj Kumar, Asha Mathur

*Chittor Vijay* (1947)
DIRECTOR: Mohan Sinha
CAST: Raj Kapoor, Madhu Bala

*Capt. Nirmala* (1947)
DIRECTOR: Om Pictures
CAST: Madan Puri

*Santosh* (1947)
DIRECTOR: Dr Mohan Sinha
CAST: Santosh Chowdhary, Madan Puri

*Ahinsa* (1946)
DIRECTOR: Ram
CAST: Navin, Mangla, Madan Puri
CHARACTER: HERO

*1857* (1946)
DIRECTOR: Mohan Sinha
CAST: Surendra, Suraiya, Madan Puri

*Imtehaan* (1946)
DIRECTOR: Madan Puri, Tasneen

*Kuldeep* (1946)
DIRECTOR: N Vaswani
CAST: Madan Puri, Vijay Mohini, Bhudo Advani

*Noor-E-Arab* (1946)
DIRECTOR: Mohan Sinha
CAST: K L Saigal, Suraiya, Madan Puri

*Pul* (1945)
DIRECTOR: Sudhir Sen
CAST: Rehana, Biman Bannerjee, Madan Puri

*Ummar Khayaam* (1945)
DIRECTOR: Mohan Sinha
CAST: K L Saigal, Suraiya, Madan Puri

*Kurukshetra* (1945)
DIRECTOR: K L Saigal, Madan Puri

*My Sister* (1944)
DIRECTOR: Hemchander Chander
CAST: K L Saigal, Sumitra Devi, Akhtar Jahan, Chandrabali Devi, Nawab, Tulsi Chakraborty, Madan Puri

*Sharda* (1942)
DIRECTOR: A R Kardar
CAST: Shyam Kumar, Amir Banu, Mehtab, Madan Puri

*Khazanchi* (1941)
DIRECTOR: Moti Gidwani
CAST: M Ismail, S D Narang, Ramola Devi, Durga Khote, Madan Puri

*Khooni Khazana*
DIRECTOR: Sheikh Mukhtiar
CAST: Sheikh Mukhtiar, Madan Puri

*Us Raat ki Baat*
CAST: Madan Puri

# ACKNOWLEDGEMENTS

Noted writers Lata Jagtiani and Manek Premchand and cine artiste and poet Tom Alter inspired me to embark on writing this biography, the compilation of which took more than seven years.

I interviewed as many of Bauji's colleagues as I could. They recalled happy memories of working with him.

I had a great meeting with Mr Ravi Chopra. He gave me photographs from all the movies of B R Films in which Bauji had acted.

Rajshree Productions gave me photographs of Bauji's movies like *Geet Gata Chal, Akhiyon ke Jharokon Se* and *Dulhan Wohi Jo Piya Man Bhaye.*

Mr Sidharth Bhatia wrote a wonderful article about the bad guys in Hindi films, with special mention of Madan Puri. His latest publication 'The Patels of Filmindia' has been well received by readers. Mr Baburao Patel had liked my father and published a nice write up on Madan Puri in the 'fifties with a centre page colour photograph.

Poet/dramatist/actor Vivek Tandon put me in touch with Bloomsbury Publishers.

My army colleagues General H K Sharma and Brig PM Ahluwalia, and Advocate Manjula Rao, read the penultimate draft and gave incisive comments.

My younger brother director/writer Ramnesh who still lives in my parents' home, shared a wealth of photographs. Since he had always lived with my parents, he was able to relate many anecdotes.

Discussions with family members sharpened hazy memories of our growing up years. My daughters, Kanchan and Sonal, revisited childhood memories. Kanchan provided office space and facilities to carry out my research. Swati Chowkekar of Kanchan's office was of invaluable assistance. Sonal's home in California was the venue for the most major edit in 2013. Anoop Puri (son of Chaman tayaji) shared his collection of photographs of tayaji and the family.

My wife Jane was a great support in the entire process of getting the material together. She also helped in restructuring the book so that it read smoothly.

Ms Himanjali Sankar, Commissioning Editor of Bloomsbury Publishing India Pvt Ltd gave my confidence a boost by accepting my manuscript and promising to make it a book to be proud of. My meeting with Mr Rajiv Beri, MD of Bloomsbury was equally encouraging.

I have enjoyed every moment of the writing of this biography. Any shortcomings are wholly mine.

Thank you Bauji, for the opportunity to get to know you better.

K K PURI